WARP-SPEED SPEED BRANDING

Adweek Books is designed to present interesting, insightful books for the general business reader and for professionals in the worlds of media, marketing, and advertising.

These are innovative, creative books that address the challenges and opportunities of these industries, written by leaders in the business. Some of our writers head their own companies, whereas others have worked their way up to the top of their field in large multinationals. They share, however, a knowledge of their craft and a desire to enlighten others.

We hope readers will find these books as helpful and inspiring as *Adweek*, *Brandweek*, and *Mediaweek* magazines.

Published

Disruption: Overturning Conventions and Shaking Up the Marketplace, Jean-Marie Dru

Under the Radar: Talking to Today's Cynical Consumer, Jonathan Bond & Richard Kirshenbaum

Truth, Lies and Advertising: The Art of Account Planning, Jon Steel

Hey, Whipple, Squeeze This!: A Guide to Creating Great Ads, Luke Sullivan

Eating the Big Fish: How Challenger Brands Can Compete Against Brand Leaders, Adam Morgan

Warp-Speed Branding: The Impact of Technology on Marketing, Agnieszka Winkler

Creative Company: How St. Luke's Became "The Ad Agency to End All Ad Agencies," Andy Law

WARP- SPEED BRANDING

the impact of technology on marketing

AGNIESZKA WINKLER

John Wiley & Sons, Inc.

New York • Chichester • Weinheim • Brisbane • Singapore • Toronto

To my husband and soul mate, Arthur K. Lund,
who exhibits much patience with me and all my escapades.

This book is printed on acid-free paper. ♾

Copyright © 1999 by Agnieszka Winkler. All rights reserved.
Published by John Wiley & Sons, Inc.

Published simultaneously in Canada.

This publication is designed to provide accurate and authoritative information in
regard to the subject matter covered. It is sold with the understanding that the
publisher is not engaged in rendering legal, accounting, or other professional
services. If legal advice or other expert assistance is required, the services of a
competent professional person should be sought.

Library of Congress Cataloging-in-Publication Data:
Winkler, Agnieszka.
    Warp-speed branding : the impact of technology on marketing / by
Agnieszka Winkler.
       p.   cm.
    "Adweek books."
    Includes index.
    ISBN 0-471-29555-8 (cl. : alk. paper)
    1. Brand name products—Marketing—Management. 2. Marketing—
Technological innovations. 3. High technology—Marketing.
I. Title.
HF5415.13.W548   1999
658.8'27—dc21   99-12222
                                                       CIP

Printed in the United States of America.

10 9 8 7 6 5 4 3 2 1

Contents

Today, technology is impacting almost every industry. The role of innovation is increasing and product life cycles are shrinking. Massive amounts of information at our connected fingertips, combined with immense time compression, are forcing brand builders to look for new solutions. To thrive in this warp-speed world, companies need to adopt new ways to communicate and collaborate as they make decisions about their brands.

Consumers are changing, shaped by social forces and the power of technology. They are more informed, more demanding, and more skeptical. They increasingly hold brand power! We examine lessons learned from the technology world on how to shape a brand in this consumer-centric world, and how the brand can be a powerful anchor in fast-changing environments.

Explore the six myths of branding: "A brand is built over a long time," "Advertising is the major creator of a brand," "The brand needs a manager," and more. Then look at the six branding truths of the warp-speed world—new principles that shatter the old myths.

Are your product life cycles shortening? Are new kinds of alliances forming in your industry? Do your employees have access to the Internet? Then read about impediments to branding that these cause, and how to deal with them; the new skills you'll need in your workforce; and the changes in attitude and processes you'll need to adapt to the warp-speed world.

As the world of marketing and branding evolves, ad agencies must rethink many of their own processes and mindsets to be truly valuable to their clients. We'll look at ways to use technology to streamline advertising development and to help clients achieve faster time to market.

Learn about TeamToolz™, a sophisticated web-centric application designed to help clients manage the workflow of multiple agencies and synchronize their activities to get to market faster.

We introduce the concept of the Brand Ecosystem, the increasingly complex set of interrelationships of all the stakeholders and brands involved in pulling together a product or service. These multiple constituencies complicate the brand definition. Find concrete actions to help you be more successful in defining your Brand Ecosystem and managing it for the benefit of your brand.

Chapter 8 **Warp-Speed Branding and the Internet:**   **163**
How It Relates to the New Marketing Reality

The Internet is emerging as a vital direct link from producer to con-
sumer, and the rate of Internet adoption by consumers is unprece-
dented. In the process, the Internet is changing the fundamentals of
the brand experience. We examine the facts of brand life on the Inter-
net and suggest some approaches to taking advantage of this powerful
new force.

Chapter 9 **The Brand Audit as a Tool for a Fast-Moving World**   **179**

Brand audits are nothing new. The world of technology, however, has
required us to change our brand assessment approach to take into
account the fundamental nature of technology markets and the impact
of technology innovations. Learn the lessons from our experience with
companies like Tektronix and CyberStar.

Chapter 10 **How Ready Are You for Warp-Speed Branding?**   **201**

Is "time to market" a concept that's known throughout your com-
pany? Does marketing have access to customer information? Do your
agencies talk to each other regularly? Answer these and 28 other ques-
tions to help you determine your readiness for warp-speed branding.

Preface

Move Over P&G: High Tech Isn't What You Think

Technology and branding—it isn't a subject you're likely to hear about at cocktail parties. Mix technology and branding and you get a weird kind of drink, maybe like that wheat grass stuff that was so popular here in northern California. It is, however, a combo that plenty of the geeks, the rich geeks in Silicon Valley, love. You know them. They are driving either 20-year-old Volvos with huge rust spots, or shiny new Porsche Boxsters in beautiful silver. For the most part, they are fanatical about technology and blasé about the kind of money the industry has made in the last 10 years. Many have enough stock options to send entire families to graduate school, but would still rather sit in front of their computers and eat pizza than go to a five-star restaurant. There are many contradictions about the world they have created, but one thing is for sure—it is they who are producing hundreds of millions of dollars in revenue and billions of dollars in value for the new Knowledge Economy. Of course, they don't have to wear suits.

These have been my clients for the last 15 years. They have provided me with many opportunities to build whole new industries, to explore new markets, and to challenge conventional marketing thought.

The very first connection I had with technology was about 20 years ago. I was finishing my masters degree in history, and I picked up a consulting job with Fairchild Semiconductor, whose most notable spin-offs include Intel and LSI Logic. They were getting involved in eastern European business and the chairman, Lester Hogan, was looking for someone who could talk with his senior executives about doing business in eastern Europe. As I speak Polish and Russian and had visited the eastern bloc on several occasions, I got the job. That was my first introduction to the world of technology.

I didn't start in advertising; I started in the credit department of a technology company. Soon after that, by happenstance, I did get a job in a small ad agency in Palo Alto, which at the time was just starting to see the emergence of Silicon Valley. Nine months later, I hung out my own shingle with my first client, Perkin Elmer Ultek, a semiconductor equipment manufacturer. That started an advertising practice that has had an emphasis on high tech and has allowed the company to grow into a leading West Coast agency billing $80 million.

In the first five years or so of my career, I didn't realize I was dealing with a special type of client. It wasn't until about 12 years ago when we picked up our first consumer client, Schlage Lock, that I realized not everyone moved with what I have come to call a warp-speed work style. Over time, we've built a list of both technology-driven and non-technology-focused clients. In the last few years, I've noticed that even nontechies have begun to exhibit all the stresses of my technology clients. Product cycles have shortened. Consumers have become more demanding and elusive. Competition—because of technology—has become more cutthroat.

The Contrast Has Never Been More Apparent

The purpose of this book is to uncover some of the forces of technology that are ripping apart the world of branding, advertising, and marketing. The contrast between the way brand building has traditionally been done and the way it is emerging have never been more apparent. Think back to those black-and-white days when any attempts to change or modulate a household brand like Tide was done with great care and trepidation. All eyes were focused on the product and the package. The color of the box was more important than how the customers lived their lives. It took many years for Warner Lambert to take Listerine and extend the mouthwash brand to toothpaste. The brand may have been king, but it was conservative and change was managed very carefully by the brand management team alone. In contrast, the Apple Computer brand was built in less than 10 years and has extended over a variety of machines such as Apple II, the Mac Classic, the Quadra, the PowerPC, PowerBook, and the iMac, to name just a few. Microsoft built its operating system brand in 12 years, and in the process built itself into a business with market valuation equal to General Motors. Microsoft extended its brand power over all kinds of software, content, and services. It has even managed to put its imprint on a cable television channel, MSNBC, and word that CEO Bill Gates is coming draws crowds rivaling those of a rock star.

Yahoo! and Amazon.com are on-line companies that built their brands in months, not years! The implications of this warp speed are phenomenal. To be successful in this new environment, companies must organize differently to deliver products and services at an unprecedented clip. Time to market is now the operating phrase and the role of the brand must be viewed differently in an ever-churning world. The consumer and the employee are different animals today, simultaneously shaped by and shaping the new Knowledge Economy. We are no longer the linear, process-oriented, rational world of the Industrial Revolution.

Rather, we are fluid, networked, and intuitive. The tried-and-true Procter & Gamble formulas for brand building are becoming increasingly irrelevant.

With this book, I'd like to challenge your thinking by making the case that new and creative ways of tackling branding have been, in fact, developed by technology companies; that the traditional ways of building brands no longer apply; that even P&G has had to rethink its classic, but perhaps outdated, methods; that the techno-geeks are, in fact, our children; that the technology culture is spreading like an amoeba throughout other businesses, even yours. You are in the technology business today. My observation, based on 20 years in advertising and marketing, is that technology's presence in every business environment changes the role of the brand builder. You will begin to see how this perspective transforms some of the standard marketing truths we all learned at the knee of consumer product giants like Procter & Gamble, Unilever, and Colgate-Palmolive. The technology companies that embody innovation and change are rewriting the rules of brand creation, and you'll see how to apply some of their lessons.

As a result of working with technology companies, some of the heretical observations we have made are that because of speed of change:

- Brand itself will be ever changing.
- Advertising is only one of the arrows in the brand-building quiver.
- Brands don't take years to build anymore.
- Brand lives in a Brand Ecosystem™.
- Brand managers no longer control the brand, and the CEO is the brand shepherd. No one really is the manager.
- Brand is *not* only a marketing concept, but also it is a financial concept, a major factor in shareholder value.

Now, have some fun with me, killing off old ideas and bringing in the new.

1

High Tech Doesn't Percolate–It Explodes

I t was late in the fall of 1995. Our client, Sony, called us down to San Jose for a hush-hush meeting about something big. We arrived full of expectation at the Sony Information Technologies of America headquarters in the heart of Silicon Valley. It had the largest lobby in Silicon Valley (a veritable Taj Mahal), the building of which was one of the last acts of Ron Sommer, the president of Sony of America, who was moved to Europe shortly afterward. Then came the exciting news. Sony was planning to enter the PC market late the following spring. Thinking this was a tight schedule to develop a great ad campaign for the launch, we immediately began asking the standard marketing plan questions: What was the product like? How much would it cost? Who was the target? Where would they buy it? How many did we need to sell? With about six months to go, we really did need to be briefed right away so that we could at least get some account planning done. The PC market was densely crowded and was undergoing some huge structural changes. How the new product was positioned would be crucial.

Well, there were to be very few concrete answers that day. The product was actually just a concept, and it existed primarily in the minds of the design team in Japan. Imagine our thoughts and emotions as it began to sink in that we were expected to begin work on an advertising campaign for a nonexistent product to an unknown target in a very complicated marketing environment. We love a challenge, but I kept thinking to myself, "This is nuts. We're never going to get this done."

During the course of several very exciting months, we worked closely with Sony as product specs and design changed on a weekly basis, as technology and manufacturing breakthroughs occurred. Software enhancements kept changing the focus of differentiation. We could not even see the physical product with its distinctive tower and purple color until March, just three short months before the launch. We weren't able to touch a working prototype until May, with ads breaking in June and the product scheduled to ship in September. All through this time the system design, product specs, and configuration alternatives were constantly changing up to the last possible second, even during the manufacturing cycle.

Welcome to Marketing in the Twenty-First Century

The complexity of this product development situation was compounded by the organizational complexity of Sony itself—a global company with multiple layers, locations, and responsibilities scattered around the world. Marketing was U.S.-based, with product marketing and advertising centered at Sony's West Coast headquarters in San Jose, California; however, there was close involvement of Sony Electronics headquarters in New Jersey. Product design work was centered in Japan, even though the product was aimed at the U.S. PC market. Our agency's recommendations on strategies and creative approaches had to be reviewed and approved by each of these constituencies. The work was seen and commented on by four major groups whose approval was needed: our primary California client, the PC-marketing team; the senior management of Sony Electronics of America; the advertising management on the East Coast; and the top-level corporate managers in Japan.

The product itself would be manufactured by Intel, not Sony, further complicating the workflow from design to production to launch and also creating branding issues, with the now famous "Intel Inside" advertising program. This complicated situation was taking place at the same time that the PC industry was facing a major "inflection" point, as Andy Grove likes to say, the sub-$1,000 PC.

It would be hard enough to introduce a *simple* product in the midst of this complex, ever changing maelstrom of product information, market information, and split responsibilities. The Sony PC situation, however, was compounded by the need to address some even more complicated issues, which Sony faced as a late entrant into the U.S. PC market:

What were we introducing? Were we simply introducing a new PC, or were we really introducing a whole new platform that would form the center of an entire Sony collection of computers, peripherals, and other devices that would work seamlessly together, like stereo equipment does? This would eventually become known as VAIO (video-audio integrated operation), but the concept was ill defined at the time.

To whom were we talking? Who was really the target consumer for a Sony product whose definition was constantly changing? Sony's entry was coming at a time in the U.S. PC market when the pace of technology change was accelerating daily. It was leading to simpler, cheaper computers that could potentially cause the home market to explode.

How would we attack the brand issues? How would the Sony brand, one of the world's most powerful, according to multiple studies done by organizations like Landor Associates and the Harris Poll, play in this new market? What could be extended from the Sony brand in consumer electronics to the new Sony PC? At the same time, what baggage existed that would make the brand extension more difficult?

How would we deal with the time crunch and the ambiguity? Finally, our biggest question: How could we launch a major campaign that would drive sales of the product for years with so little time and information?

With less than eight months from stated intent to the completed product design, manufacturing, and market launch of a complicated product into a highly unpredictable market, everyone—client, agency, manufacturing, and distribution partners—had to master a significantly different way of working together. Somehow, in this messy situation, we managed to get the job done. Even though this was the biggest project of this sort that we had ever faced, because we all were hardened warp-speed veterans, we already intuitively knew how to approach the problem.

The initial PC launch happened on schedule in the summer of 1996 at PC Expo, a major trade show in New York. The ads, which featured futuristic scenes and introduced the idea of the convergence of PCs and consumer electronics, were well received. The press gave the product decent reviews, and Sony was launched into the PC business.

It has been just about two and a half years now, and I'm writing this manuscript on my new Sony 505 subcompact. It is small, very light, and very cute. On my way back from New York, half of the airplane passengers stopped to ask me about it. I knew then this PC was going to be a big hit for Sony. A lot of learning from the initial launch of the desktop PC had gone into making this subcompact a winner.

Sony PC introductory print.

The New York Times
June 17, 1996

Sony Set to Introduce Personal Computer Line

By LAWRENCE M. FISHER

An electronic giant jumps into a growth market.

Seven months after announcing its intention to enter the personal computer business, the Sony Corporation is expected to introduce its first two machines today, designed and built in the United States for the domestic consumer market. The "PC by Sony" will cost $2,000 to $3,000, depending on features, and will be available in August, people familiar with Sony's plans said.

Given all its features, the PC would seem to offer Sony razor-thin profit margins, if any at all. Indeed, Sony executives acknowledge that the product had lower margins than they were used to, but they said the double-digit growth of the PC business made it an attractive one, and the convergence of computers, communications and entertainment was an event Sony could not afford to miss.

The PC by Sony falls short of the company's claim in November that it would produce a computer as easy to use as a television set. That prompted speculation that Sony might design its own operating system, but Sony market researc conventional i

Where Sony has put its engineering muscle is in the computer's audio and video, with a powerful amplifier and built-in speakers, and some clever software for displaying video. Indeed, the audio and video strengths would seem to set the Sony apart from earlier Japanese entries in the United States market, like Canon and Matsushita, none of which has fared well. Sony is
tion for Con
Packard, P
and other
just with it
with its str
"Becaus
the semic
ing into it
digital side
into it t
Compaq
staff writ
industry

with amazing results," he added, referring to the video display.

Packed with multimedia features and enclosed in a sleek gray-and-purple tower, Sony's PC was designed to offer entertainment features as well as powerful computing. The bare model has a 166-megahertz versior
Pentiu
bytes
megahertz
megabytes o
Sony has
"shell" inter
newcomers
erating sys
crosoft Cor
Another

THE WALL STREET JOURNAL

Sony's First PC Due Today, Priced at $2,000 to $3,000

By a WALL STREET JOURNAL Staff Reporter

NEW YORK — Sony Corp.'s entry into the personal computer market will have its debut today with an expected price of ,000 to $3,000.

The home-PC line, powered by Intel rp.'s top-of-the-line, 200-megahertz ntium chip, will offer high-quality ind and graphics but isn't radically 'erent from other computers on the rket. Complete with a 28.8-kilobit-per->nd modem, the dark gray computers provide owners with a direct

HOUSTON CHRONICLE

HOUSTON, TX
DAILY   416,004
TUESDAY
JUN 18 1996

BURRELLE'S

Powerful multimedia PC unveiled by Sony

By DWIGHT SILVERMAN
Houston Chronicle

NEW YORK   Sony Electronics on Monday took the wraps off its highly anticipated entry into the home computer mark-

chief operating officer of Sony Electronics, and the two models Sony is introducing won't be available until late August, and pricing has not yet been set but will be in the $2,000 to $3,000 range

first time Intel has openly partnered with a computer maker.

The computer also is the latest attempt by a Japanese company to grab a share of the worldwide PC market, which is dominated by American firms. Other Japanese firms, such as NEC, have tried and failed to become dominant players in the bus
merged its
erations wi
based Pack
When it's
Sony will fe
■ Pentiur
at 166 and
■ Config
and 32 meg
cess memo
■ The 3
made by A
megabytes
■ Large
from 2.1 to
■ A 28,80
feature tha

another PC and talk on the phone over the same line. Sony hopes to use this to help with technical support calls, Yankowski said.
■ Three-dimensional sound built into a Sony Trinitron monitor, complete with a subwoofer built into the stand.

San Francisco Examiner
June 17, 1996

Sony unveils PC line

Electronics giant's new bid to keep up with digital age

By Margaret D. Williams
BLOOMBERG BUSINESS NEWS

NEW YORK — Sony Corp. will unveil its first line of personal computers Monday, throwing the weight of one of the world's most-recognized names into the $116 billion-a-year global PC market.

The company that brought the world the first transistor radio and Walkman music player is betting the PC will become as common in homes as the television or stereo. It is introducing the machines in the States the largest comput-

chief news confer-
Sony Music Studios
sts such as Michael
Bruce Springsteen
1 – the PC by Sony
to a standing-room-
hat, at one point,
) the street. Among
re both U.S. and
executives.
ony is a joint ven-
iny and Intel Corp.,
he processor and
m board for the
has been provid-
irds, or mother-
anufacturers for
C by Sony is the

CHICAGO SUN-TIMES

CHICAGO, IL
DAILY   523,709
TUESDAY
JUN 18 1996

BURRELLE'S

Sony unveils its first PC

NEW YORK—In the most anticipated entry into tl personal computer market this year, Sony Corp. u: veiled its first PC, bringing its reputation and a touch purple to an industry many perceive as unfriendly ar colorless. Since last fall, when Sony declared its inten tion to enter the PC business, the company's fir products have been awaited as a sign of a future i which computers are designed more like stereos an TVs. The first models demonstrate that Sony is tryii to be part of the PC mainstream. A color scheme wit

Soon after we became immersed in the launch planning for the original desktop and notebook PC, I had lunch with a good friend who is the director of advertising for a large international bank. Over dessert, she described a situation at her bank in which she was wrestling with a product change at the same time that her customer was changing. There were some tricky marketing conditions, and all of this was in the midst of swirling rumors about mergers and acquisitions, but with no clarity about who was doing the acquiring. Decisions, however, had to be made now, and time to market was short. Her situation in the banking world sounded eerily like our Sony PC launch. After that lunch, I began to realize that what we thought was endemic to technology companies might, in fact, be a much broader condition affecting much of global business today. If that were true, then the learnings we had amassed from years of dealing with these types of situations should be looked at and codified, so our wealth of experience could become valuable information for others who were just beginning to encounter some of the same issues.

This was reinforced a couple of weeks later in a casual meeting with several professors at the Leavey School of Business of Santa Clara University. They described their work with retailers and packaged-goods marketers as well as other technology-based companies. I began to see similarities with our Sony experience, my friend's banking situation, and the professors' experiences: rapid technology developments; the need for concurrent development of product, marketing, and distribution plans in the midst of the constantly shifting sands of information; and the critical importance, but great difficulty, of coordinating far-flung teams and keeping everyone up-to-date with the very latest information.

I realized that just about every industry, not just high technology, was in the same boat, and that the fundamental factors of innovation and abundance of information were, in fact, changing the entire landscape of marketing. They were responsible for a time compression, which produced a series of major effects that, when recognized, became easier to deal with.

Time Compression

We are living in a sliver of time during which 10 years has redefined the concept of fast food from a drive-through McDonald's to a 30-second microwave meal; nail polish dries in 30 seconds; photos are developed in one hour; and money comes out of street-corner machines instantly. We haven't even used the word *computer*, yet!

We no longer think of FedEx as a big deal. Even faxing is cumbersome as we tap in our passwords on voice mail and e-mail. Of course, there is almost no time or patience left for paper-based correspondence, or "snail mail" as it is fondly referred to around Silicon Valley.

Now, when we want to reach someone, we page them, and we are quite irritated if they don't respond immediately. If we want information, we command a search engine from our desk to find what we want on the World Wide Web—no need to get in a car, drive down to the library, and ask our friendly librarian if she could please help us. With technology at our fingertips, we can help ourselves. We can do it *now*, which means "24-7": 24 hours a day, 7 days a week.

If there is an initial launching pad for technology companies to battle for leadership in the iconography of brand building, it is pure and simple: It is *speed*.

This isn't speed in its relative sense, for example, driving 65 miles per hour in a 30-mile-per-hour zone. Rather, it is an exponential explosion that deconstructs our sensory system and replaces it with an entirely new set of structures. On the surface, it is replacing a dial telephone with a series of push buttons, while underneath it is the technologic transformation from analog systems to digital networks. It's as simple as filling out your FedEx form, while underneath it's a package distribution system involving hundreds of airplanes, thousands of trucks, and an extremely sophisticated satellite-based computer tracking system.

Terrorists can blow up an American embassy in Nairobi, and within minutes the President of the United States is watching a live report on CNN—faster than he could have received a "sitrep" from the CIA or the State Department. A hospital can get an electronic report on trauma victims at an accident scene and begin treatment long before a patient is transported to an emergency ward, saving previously unsavable lives. Machines can be taught to perform a task with robotics—and even work all night in workerless factories.

A graduate student at the University of California in Berkeley can access the virtual stacks of libraries all over the world and arrange for them to lend him or her important research materials—all without leaving their carrel at Green Library. A mother can learn that her daughter may have fallen victim to a rare disease, and within minutes learn of possible cures and research going on around the globe, as well as tie into a virtual support group of parents facing similar crises, all before she goes to consult a specialist.

It isn't necessary to understand in detail how this shift took place, but it is relevant to have a sense of the enormous impact of the knowledge revolution on the way we work and learn—and even play—as we move into the new millennium.

Consider that your products and their pricing may be obsolete by the end of the next quarter. Think about the impact of a new competitor who can produce the same product in a way that is barely distinguishable from your own, but at a lower price and the same quality. Try finding a computer company staking its future on machines that use Intel's old chips. Maybe there is an overnight shipper that isn't using the latest bar coding technology. It is now dangerous to be behind the technology curve. Whether you are a customer or a producer, the pace of innovation is so swift that shorter and shorter product cycles place even greater pressure on the one thing that does stick around—the brand.

But Wait, Technology Has Nothing to Do with My Business

Technology today is so pervasive, it affects everything we do and everyone in almost every field of endeavor, whether we like it or not. Think of textiles while you thumb through the latest fashion catalogs. New types of technology innovations are stimulating the creation of new high-tech fabrics that enable all kinds of never-before-seen clothing designs. Velvet swimwear may not be essential to the health and well-being of the planet, but it is a high-tech application offering the brand builder the chance to differentiate an otherwise plain old bathing suit in the oldest of industries, fashion. My satin stretch pants will never bag or sag due to a special polymer that has been added to the fabric. My state-of-the-art golf clubs have titanium heads, which I am convinced have improved my game. On a recent trip to Los Angeles, our Hertz car had a Magellan GPS-based pathfinder. We punched in our address and a map popped up showing our current location. As we moved, the virtual car on the map moved and a voice told us when to move right or left for the next turn. One hour, 4 freeways, and 10 side streets later, we were at our hotel. In the fall of 1998, Acura began advertising new models that included this feature built-in.

My Volant skis are made with a stainless-steel cap to improve their performance. My Gore-Tex shoes keep my feet dry in the rain. What's on the horizon? Bottles that give an expiration date based not only on age, but on temperature, humidity, or light? Tiny sensors to remind you when to take your pills? Detergent packaging that communicates with washing machines to determine at what temperature to wash certain clothes, or how much detergent to use? How about a chip embedded under the skin that monitors the level of glucose in the blood and transmits the data to a watch-like receiver for diabetes sufferers?

These are everyday applications of technology that give owners a new experience. In fact, the high-technology components of these consumer products are sometimes the main feature of the brand. High-performance gasoline, as well as motor oil, rely on superior performance through the application of new technology, and they brand the technology itself. Chevron's Techron is one example in which the brand is linked with a technology advance. Do consumers even know how Techron gasoline is different from regular gasoline? Probably not, but they know it is the result of new technology, and that is viewed as a powerful piece of Chevron's brand value. Even in shampoo commercials, Pantene vitamin enrichers are seen to be a high-tech aid for damaged hair. We have already been taught as consumers, that damaged hair will damage our love lives. Real or not, that's how technology is being used to enhance the brand in everyday consumer products.

Technology has even invaded our bedrooms today. Pfizer's drug Viagra, a product of innovation in biotechnology, is an example of an innovation that is designed to enhance male and female sexual performance. Want better sex? We have the latest technology, and you don't have to bring it home in a brown-paper bag. Want to decide the sex of your child? You can now. There is literally no piece of our lives that has not been touched by the power of technology.

Faster New Product Development

Technological innovations have been infiltrating some of the most traditional industrial businesses for some time now. The primary beneficiary is almost always the consumer. In 1992, the Honda Accord was the top-selling car in the United States for the third year in a row. Following close behind—with the gap closing rapidly—was the Ford Taurus. In 1993, however, the new Accord blew Taurus out of the water. How? By introducing a totally redesigned car for that model year and leaping ahead in sales. Was this new product introduction due to luck? Coincidence? Years of careful planning and committee meetings? Hardly. What really happened was that the U.S.-based Honda design center began to work on the new Accord in 1991, a mere two years before launch. Honda executives in Japan could track the potential decline in Accord sales a few years out and develop new product attributes and cost-cutting measures to make the Accord competitive for years to come.

Now, you might ask if this two-year new-product development cycle—versus what at the time was a four- to five-year cycle for American manufacturers—was really due to Honda's technological sophistication, or its favorable labor relations, or its just-in-time manufacturing process. In reality, it wasn't any of those factors individually. It really was due to the *implementation* of technology, along with a collaborative work style and other factors, which gave Honda and most Japanese automobile manufacturers a huge competitive advantage over their American counterparts.

In fact, if you look closely, the similarities in the challenges facing both Honda and the "Big Three" American auto companies were striking. First of all, over 80 percent of all Honda Accords were, and still are, built in a plant in Marysville, Ohio. In fact, a large percentage of Accords built in Marysville are exported for sale in Japan. Most of the workers are career autoworkers, having come from Ford and GM plants across the Ohio River. Even the production process was a holdover from the assembly-line system, which was perfected by Henry Ford when he built the Model T. No team-building, Saturn-style assembly plant here—just one long moving line of cars with workers at individual workstations.

How did Honda, operating under essentially the same environment as its competitors, implement technology to its advantage? When the Southern California Design Center notified Japanese headquarters about its recommendation to redesign the car, Honda's collaborative style sprang into action. To operate under such a drastically reduced cycle time, the designers in California needed to work concurrently with the engineers in Japan and the manufacturing people in Ohio. Decisions often needed to be made in tandem, without much time for deliberation. In fact, the design center personnel who acted as the team leaders on this project frequently worked in shifts, operating on a 24-hour-per-day basis.

To streamline the manufacturing process, Honda implemented a true just-in-time delivery process. All parts suppliers were linked electronically to the manufacturing schedule, so that they could see well in advance when their respective parts were due. The brake pad manufacturer, for example, received his order in enough time to have product available exactly when each car's brakes were to be installed. By *exactly*, I mean within hours, not days or weeks, of the time it was needed on the assembly line. In return for this direct computer link, which would allow each supplier to regulate its own manufacturing, suppliers had to guarantee delivery of the parts to the precise day. Not only did this minimize the amount of product that needed to be warehoused, but it drastically cut inventory costs for Honda. It also forced everyone involved in the process—designers, engineers, parts suppliers—to work and think in sync. The ultimate benefit of this technology to consumers was that a brand new Honda Accord was available much sooner than anyone expected, at virtually no increase in sticker price.

At about the same time, Porsche Cars A.G., based in Stuttgart, Germany, hired Japanese consultants to come in and overhaul their production processes. This was extremely controversial with employees and customers alike. This iconic German sports car manufacturer, known for fine hand-crafted automobiles, was inviting foreigners in to tell them how to build cars. For critics, it looked as if robots might be taking over. For Porsche management, however, it was more a matter of survival. The recession in the early 1990s reduced sales of the 911 (the company's flagship model), and manufacturing costs and sticker prices were spiraling out of control. Porsche, which was enjoying sales of over 30,000 units in the heady days of the late 1980s, was faced with selling fewer than 5,000 in 1993.

The recommendation from the consultants was to keep most of the hand-crafted manufacturing process, but to radically alter the inventory management and delivery systems. Parts became available literally just when the worker needed them, reducing confusion and clutter on the factory floor. Inventory costs were slashed. Because of the efficiencies of being linked to its suppliers via computer, there was much clearer communication and stronger relationships with suppliers than ever before. Again, the main benefit of this implementation of technology was that in 1995, when Porsche introduced an evolution of its 911 (internally called the 993), the car was faster and braked in a shorter distance than any 911. The list price was more than $6,000 less than that of the previous year's model.

With both Porsche and Honda, technology greatly improved their businesses, but it wasn't the technology alone that made the difference. Both companies were open to using technology in a different way that would alter the conventional work style of their employees.

Unquestionably, technology has dramatically changed our lives as businesspeople, as consumers, and as brand builders.

Here's How We Got Here: Social Forces Greet Technology

So how did these powerful forces that are changing how we live, work, and play come about?

The Cold War, now long forgotten, produced an unprecedented stream of new technology that has been continuously commercialized over the past 50 years. New inventions have been appearing at an amazing clip, and the consumer's appetite for what is new and different has been stimulated to a gargantuan proportion. We are now our own Godzilla when it comes to technology consumption.

In the late 1960s, our mothers started going to work en masse, leaving us to amuse ourselves with the TV and, later, video games. I grew up listening to the radio while I did my homework. My kids grew up to the sound and quick cuts of MTV. This taught us as a society that concentration can be split. There may be three TVs going and no one is really watching them because they are involved in other activities. As a matter of fact, we can now steer three tons of steel down the freeway at 70 miles per hour and dial a phone while we mentally prepare the points in our presentation and pick up our voice mail. Of course, such multitasking at the wheel is not recommended and does cause its fair share of accidents.

Younger generations are used to doing several things at once. In fact, they crave it. Just as they amused themselves with TV and video games while they did their homework, some of your employees may want to work with the radio on.

The day-to-day work routine is being made more flexible in progressive companies to accommodate a cycle that is less and less 9-to-5. With the advent of the laptop, it is commonplace for work and playtime to be mixed up in a jumble, for which even physical location offers no clear distinction. In our agency offices, people play their individual boom boxes or run music or music videos through their computers, even though we have an open, no-walls environment. Those who want to tune out the white noise do so electronically with headphones. Firing up a computer late at night at home to check on e-mail is as normal nowadays as the three-martini lunch was a decade or two ago. Secretaries have been replaced by voice mail. Our agency staff all have access to the same network remotely, so that they can work at home, on the road, or out on our sundeck if they want to enjoy the view. In return for working extra hours off-site, they may choose to play games or shop on the Web during the so-called traditional office hours, which is fine in our office as long as the work gets done.

The concept of work and play is blurring, as consumer focus groups tell us. This is not only because some work is done at home after hours and some play is done in the office during working hours. It also comes from the blending of content. Entertainment and instruction are coming together in the form of video and computer games. For example, financial companies are building simulation games to instruct their new interns. This makes sense, because there is no longer the time in our warp-speed society to train and mentor new employees, one-on-one, as there was in the past.

The idea that work is fun is probably one of the most difficult for traditional managers to embrace. The MTV generation, however, sees it differently. A less formal workplace, a more casual acceptance of traditional roles in the office, and a greater desire to have work be something cool—all are the direct results of the way the new workforce has grown up and the interconnectivity of the computer. The computer's ability to offer all kinds of scenario-playing games has turned the job into another game to be played to see who can conquer the world. The ability of the computer to transform real-world events into games that can be experienced with little physical danger has offered an entire generation of new workers the chance to see work as a game, not as servile drudgery.

In my college days, we still typed our own term papers. If we needed to make an edit, we had to retype not just paragraphs, but whole sections. Today, working on this book, I'm cutting and pasting, writing and rewriting, simultaneously on my computer. Thinking and execution are coming together. They are no longer sequential activities. The new generation, more accustomed to tools that allow them to do tasks concurrently, wants to work that way. Sequential processes are considered boring and slow, and more important, an impediment to freethinking and creativity. If we do two things at once, naturally, we'll get done faster, won't we?

Maybe with the random choice of which two things we do at once, we'll discover something new and interesting. That would be cool—and *cool* is the Holy Grail.

Do you remember the first time you figured out how to program the speed-dial function on your phone? No big deal, right? Well, for most people born before 1970, the speed of technological change has been daunting. Anyone who did not grow up typing on a keyboard, clicking with a mouse, or moving a joystick around is confronted with a whole set of real physical challenges that tests their eye-hand coordination, as well as their mental acuity in a world in which *nanosecond* is an everyday term. Today, however, as baby boomers who grew up on Pac-Man move into middle age, and all the generations who follow them move into adulthood, we are suddenly becoming a society in which the majority, not the minority, are technologically literate.

Generations that grew up practicing eye-hand coordination don't like to sit in long meetings, to write text memos, or to constantly work and rework the same project. Rather, they prefer a loose environment; quick, impromptu meetings on sofas or at patio tables; e-mail communication whenever possible because it's instantaneous and because you get to click something. Some Silicon Valley companies have installed slides between floors, and one company in the San Francisco multimedia gulch even sports a fireman's pole to get people down from floor to floor. The environment is *kinetic*, for people who need to do and think simultaneously. If you are not used to it, a better choice of words would be *frenetic*.

There's more. Social changes have impacted work styles in other ways as well. The nuclear family has blown up, and with it has gone the authority figure of the traditional family. Add that to the impact of the computer, which has essentially democratized information, and you find that the traditional chain of command does not work for the new knowledge worker. They were not used to authority at home as they spent more time on their own with both parents working, and they don't especially like it at the office either. Freethinking, with access to all kinds of information, it becomes harder and harder to box these people into tight-fitting jobs with linear processes—they just don't work that way very well.

The age of the corporation organized along the principles of mass manufacturing, a linear process, and chain of command is over. Remember, there is no draft anymore, no boot camp, no training in chain-of-command behavior and obedience to your superiors. The generations for which video games, action movies, and MTV are normal have little regard for the rules of behavior in the corporate environment. The phenomenal success of technology companies has shown them that corporate ladders don't create innovation and value. They have little trouble absorbing the skills necessary to operate in human hyperspeed, and they feel quite confident in their ability to pick up and work elsewhere. They demand the latest and greatest in technologic resources and, to a large extent, they get it. High-speed data transmission lines are a must; access to computers and computer technology is essential. How else can you do 16 things at once?

The insatiable desire for the new and the now makes the worker of the new economy gravitate to technology-driven companies, because they behave exactly the same way.

New Ways of Organizing Work–Must I Hire a Massage Therapist, Too?

Concurrent. Collaborative. Integrated. Intuitive. Fluid. These are words that to our one-minute manager, samurai strategists' ears sound very California, very "new agey." By that, I mean laid back, casual, friendly. It also tends to mean not particularly competitive or very bottom-line oriented. But now, I'm going to say "Cisco, Hewlett-Packard, Intel, Microsoft, Apple." These are companies that stand for billions of dollars in sales and trillions of dollars in shareholder value. These companies are competitive as hell, and they are masters of playing Beat the Clock—the time-to-market clock—even though they use many new-age processes in their workplace.

How do they do it? The secret may be in the different work style they have adopted—one that fits more naturally with the cultural bent of this young workforce, one that is highly dependent on a networked information flow made possible by the computer, and one that gets them to market in unbelievably short time periods. Ascend Communications, one of the agency's clients before its acquisition by Lucent, can routinely roll out products to market in three months or less, from design through development to manufacturing to first customer ship. The agency even coined the phrase "Ascend Time" to memorialize the breakneck speed at which we worked for this client. We used to think our clients were crazy, but we've learned a lot from them, even though mastering the new tempo has been hard on our nervous systems.

Increasingly, this is how work is getting done, not only in technology companies, but in many industries slowly being overtaken by the new forces of change. The fashion industry, for instance, holds its runway shows in Milan or Paris; a month later, the low-priced, ready-to-wear knockoff is available at your local T. J. Maxx. Some years ago, we had a French cosmetics client called Den Beauté. They had developed a manufacturing process that allowed them to make lipstick, eye shadow, and nail polish in fashion colors coordinated to the new fall and spring lines and have them in the stores within weeks of the spring and fall fashion shows.

Bank customers now expect their loans to be approved in one day. Bank of America responded by launching its speedy approval process and the whole concept of on-line banking as a point of differentiation. Airline travelers keep changing their travel itineraries, and the airline industry developed the electronic ticket. Now, instead of asking the travel agency to write out tickets for

---

Traditional versus Contemporary
Company Characteristics

THE TRADITIONAL COMPANY	THE CONTEMPORARY COMPANY
Sequential processes	Concurrent processes
Hierarchical organization	Collaborative organization
Departmentalized work	Integrated work
Rational decision making	Intuitive decision making
Process-driven	Fluid in nature

---

you and messenger or overnight them to your office, you just call or click and go.

Wherever consumer demand for the new and the now intersects with technology capability, you will be sure to find the new ways of working. If you aren't adopting some of these new ways yet, you can be sure your competitor is. With these new demands comes the requirement that marketers reduce their time to market. These new pressures, driven by speed, create the need for a whole new set of skills embodied in what I call *warp-speed branding*.

2

Technology Impacts Branding: The Changing Consumer

W ork styles are changing dramatically, but that's not all that's changing. It's no accident that the people making technology happen are the same ones who grew up in the visually rich, adrenaline-pumping environment of MTV music videos, point-and-click computers, and ATMs. These young people are already part of the technology culture. They have been shaped and influenced by its power, and they define the new consumer. We all know the homemaker is no longer at home, but out working the second family job, while the children are creating web pages their parents don't even understand.

At a focus group last fall, I was struck by a response from one of the women in the group. Asked what communications devices she used, she answered that she had a computer at the office, a laptop at home, a pager, a Palm computer, and a cell phone. She had a great deal of enthusiasm for all of these "modern conveniences." Then she paused reflectively and commented: "Sometimes I feel like I'm on an electronic leash." She's right, of course, but that leash just keeps getting shorter and shorter as the new consumer insists on being in touch at all times.

My own daughter and her husband are a working, professional couple with demanding jobs in Silicon Valley's do-it-now culture. With two dogs, a toddler, and a brand new baby, their lives are complicated. Their lifestyle bears little resemblance to most of the commercials we see about family life. Time is the most precious of commodities. Service—in the sense of delivery at any hour of the day or night—is prized. They don't care about Tidy Bowl or which brand of detergent is being used. Walk into their home and the first thing you notice is the big-screen TV, which is often on as white noise, and the two laptops on the sofa, next to the portable phones that my grandson loves to play with. They are the consummate DINTs, a growing consumer category that we call "dual income, no time."

Partially because of this lack of time, partially because of the availability of technology, as prices keep declining and products get easier to use, instant gratification is no longer something to be embarrassed about. Blame it on MTV with its ad campaign of "I want my MTV" if you want, but the demanding consumer is a way of life. It is on-line banking, 24-hour supermarkets, Sunday shopping at the mall, and touch-tone movie tickets. Advances and access to technology have led people to expect products and services to be available anytime, anywhere. They need them to be in order to juggle all the things they have chosen to juggle.

This desire for instant gratification is doing more than just making young people impatient. It is revolutionizing the relationship between the consumer and the brand. It is no longer enough to have a good product, with a carefully crafted brand image delivered through advertising. Now, how someone feels about a brand is also affected by the immediacy of fulfillment. The new brand promise is about much more than just product appeal. It now must address delivery (preferably to our doorstep), postsale support, the convenience of returns (we're likely to change our minds), and perks if we buy again. Basically, the new brand promise is about the sum total of our experience with and around the whole product or service experience, in the broadest sense.

I'm a confessed catalog shopper. The mailman probably gets a hernia delivering catalogs to our doorstep. As I live in a co-op, I've noticed that I'm not the only one. Over the last year, I've also noticed that a number of catalog companies have now instituted free postage for returns—the last objection I may have had to catalog shopping. Not only can I get my errands done while watching *The Practice* at 10:00 at night, I won't have to lug them home. They arrive in a day or two—in most cases, more quickly than I could have found time to get to the store. If I don't like something, the return shipping label, postage-paid, is included. I can just pop it back in the box with less effort than trying to find a parking space in San Francisco.

Dell Computers, for example, the mass manufacturer of PCs, is now able to offer customized machines directly to the consumer because of sophisticated, just-in-time assembly and direct delivery. This almost instant build-to-order model is a business breakthrough, and it has become a major differentiator for the Dell brand. Dell is able to take advantage of a highly automated manufacturing process to connect directly with its consumer in a way that appears unique and personal. In addition, Dell and some of its competitors have been able to devise a first-rate service system that either helps fix a problem by contact with a telephone technician or provides the customer with a new computer. The offer of choice and total customer satisfaction, without having to pay a premium, conveys a sense of partnership, which has made Dell a wildly successful company and has strengthened the relationship with the customer—the ultimate bond of the brand. Meanwhile, Dell has been able to eliminate the retail channel—enabling it to improve its margins without losing its competitive edge.

Along with the ability to do it yourself any hour of the day or night comes a sense of individual supremacy that is changing the way people relate to their brands. The "me, me, me" generation is always ready to go shopping.

Just as young workers place a greater emphasis on their individual achievements, so young consumers respond to brands that offer them individual attention. The same attitude about work, for which there is little corporate loyalty, is extended to the marketplace. Self-reliance is reinforced because no one expects to stay with the same company for many years. Certainly, few companies today offer a fat retirement salary. What you put into your 401(K) will have to get you through. Like young consumers, young workers have very limited loyalty, except to things they find interesting and fun. That's just one of the many changing behaviors that successful brand builders have to tap into to establish a real connection with the new worker.

Let's return to the new consumer for a moment. Because of greater access to information, the consumer is more informed than ever before. Ten years ago, when we went shopping at the supermarket, we might have looked at the weight of a package and the price to see if it was a good deal. Today, we check for additives, the exact fat content, the grams of carbohydrates, and even which sugar substitute may be included. In the past, when we bought cars, we looked under the hood and perhaps checked the *Consumer Reports* ratings. Nowadays, we want to see the dealer invoice, check out car buying web sites, and haggle over what is the appropriate profit for the dealer to realize on our sale. Not so long ago, doctors were gods, not to be questioned. Now, we routinely want a second or third opinion. If we don't agree with what we hear, we'll go to our health store and self-medicate.

The point is that the consumer is much more educated today and much more skeptical. Idle product claims won't do. Word of mouth, carried electronically, can create nightmares for the best of companies. Intel had a rude awakening when a customer uncovered a small flaw with the floating point in its formidable Pentium chip. Intel initially balked at solving the problem, or even admitting it, causing a public relations nightmare. Intel's first response was that the flaw didn't matter because most customers weren't going to be affected. In the end, who won the debate? The drumbeat went out on the Internet, and Andy Grove, Intel's CEO, was forced to apologize personally. A handfull of tainted Odwalla apple juice bottles in one location became instant national news, and even with careful damage control, the brand has not yet completely recovered. The informed and skeptical consumer can easily bring down a company.

In this time-starved, information-rich society, mobile and random desires are met with mobile, on-demand solutions. Traditional store hours have been replaced by 800 numbers, catalog shopping, and on-line information and ordering. The customers can do what they want when they want. That set of expectations, such as 24-hour availability, becomes as much a part of the brand promise as the product's best features or design. Consumer expectations are increasingly built around their own needs rather than around manufacturer-created differentiation, and because of access to technology, consumers are beginning to have a bigger role in the crafting of the brand.

The End of the Old Brand Order

For at least the last 50 years, our marketing beliefs revolved around a fundamental core—that the brand was owned by the manufacturer and was built by the advertising agency. Clearly, the brand power was in the hands of the manufacturer, and advertising was the major instrument in its crafting. This belief system was born out of reality. When goods first started to be manufactured in quantity, and distribution outside of the local area became possible, the relationship with the consumer belonged exclusively to the retailer. A village grocer knew you liked unsalted butter, that you always ordered ham for Thanksgiving, and that your kids consumed two boxes of Nabisco crackers a week. The hard goods store owner knew you were waiting for that order of yellow broadcloth to come in, that Johnny would need new shoes for the fall, and that your pump needed a replacement part every year. So without even asking, he placed the order for you.

As mass manufacturing and mass distribution became prevalent, service that depended on personal knowledge of the consumer began to disappear. What did a manufacturer 3,000 miles away know about you? What could the 30 clerks at the supermarket really know about you? As things evolved, manufacturers became aware that more direct contact with the consumer would help them predict demand and improve customer loyalty. Otherwise, the retailer would be the primary source of preference creation, because there were few other ways to get the word out. Add the national reach of radio and eventually TV, and you have the recipe for many years of very powerful brand building by manufacturers with almost no one-to-one contact with the consumer. The impact of this simple recipe on our society was phenomenal. Advertising fueled decades of free entertainment on radio and television and kept the price of newspapers and magazines so low they were easily able to build huge audiences and penetration. The now-famous soap opera became a daytime entertainment genre. Advertising became a catalog of our culture, even providing some cultural icons of its own: remember Alka-Seltzer's "Mama Mia, that's a spicy meatball!" and Wendy's "Where's the beef?"

Well-crafted advertising began to be used to build an emotional connection with the consumer. Certainly, there were distributors, dealers, rack jobbers, and retailers still lining the path; however, advertising in mass media provided a way to impact brand preference in a long and complex distribution system. At the same time, Procter & Gamble perfected the art of the brand manager—the single person responsible for crafting the brand

Advertising icons: Alka-Seltzer's "Spicy Meatballs" and Wendy's "Where's the Beef?"

and managing it through distribution to meet required volume levels.

Brand managers focused narrowly on their product, thinking about product improvements, promotions, packaging, and, most of all, advertising. A major part of the brand manager's responsibility was to develop, with the agency, new and better advertising. There were work sessions at big agencies in New York or Chicago, frequent presentations at Procter & Gamble's headquarters in Cincinnati, constant production and recall testing of new commercials. The brand manager was even formally evaluated, as part of regular personnel reviews, on his or her success in motivating the agency to produce effective advertising! Bill Green, a significant contributor to our agency's success, remembers traveling to the Benton & Bowles agency in New York to brief the creative team for a new product introduction for Zest deodorant soap based on a new color—Rose Zest—that was heading for a test market. Bill stopped at one of New York's Tie City stores and bought 15 of the most garish, rose-flowered ties he could find, as a memento for the agency team. This was a simple move aimed at bonding with the agency by creating a little fun around the project.

The manufacturer had the control of the brand in those days, and the consumers were, by and large, a far more homogeneous group than they are today. People married in their early twenties and started families right away. The men went off to work and the women took care of all the responsibilities of home life. People retired at age 65, with a pension to supplement their social security. It was a Beaver Cleaver–type of life. For marketers, the life patterns alone made decisions easier, because things were a little more constant and predictable. Minorities were demographically just that. Single-parent homes were generally unknown, as were "latchkey" kids. Middle-aged people in their fifties and sixties didn't take up aggressive sports because they were too old.

The 1960s began the breakup of our homogeneous culture, values, and institutions of the previous 50 years. The 1960s generation didn't have the shared national experiences of the Depression and World War II, which bonded people in the middle of this century. Instead, they strapped on their backpacks and attacked all corners of the globe, bringing back pieces of other cultures, such as espresso, baguettes, croissants, pita bread, and Evian and Perrier, which together eventually gave rise to a whole industry of designer water. The Vietnam War, the world's first televised war, was a painful and alienating experience, further dividing the society. Young people escaped into their personal cloud of pot smoke or LSD. Then, in the mid- to late 1970s came Pac-Man and the computer.

The consumer today is no longer a homogenous American demographic group for which the traditional brand systems had been designed, but a diverse set of individuals with very different backgrounds, relationships, tastes, needs, and interests. Just take a look at who is playing golf today. It is no longer the game for those who look like President Eisenhower. Tiger Woods is the current icon for a game from which he would have been barred on many of its prestigious courses 5 or 10 years ago. The last time I prac-ticed at the driving range in San Francisco, I stood between an African-American teenager who was being coached by a Chinese friend and an older Filipino couple. It certainly brought home the realization that, fundamentally, the world of mass manufacturing, mass distribution, and mass advertising is over. With a great push from technology, we are now in the age of mass customization, one-to-one marketing, and individualism, which has created street brands, word-of-mouth brands, and Internet brands in record time.

Technology Shifts Brand Power

Welcome to a brave new world, in which brand power has shifted away from the manufacturer to different consumer constituencies, the brand can no longer be controlled by the brand management team, and the brand has to have the freedom to breathe and change to survive.

Now, our new consumers live less by social mores and more by what feels good. They live at a much faster pace. They have greater expectations and are more self-reliant. In a wonderful after-dinner debate with a group of adults in their mid- to late twenties, I was surprised how deeply they felt that if something feels good and doesn't hurt anyone else, then it should be considered okay, no matter how much it might offend the tastes or lifestyle choices of the majority. There was a great sense of relativism. No absolutes. No higher authority. No rules. We'll each decide for ourselves in every situation, whether it's a moral or ethical decision. We'll certainly decide what to believe about a product, and advertising will not hoodwink us.

Our new consumers are bombarded with advertising at the very same time that they are bombarded with information. All that information is available because of technology. Over the last decade cable has reached 60-percent-plus penetration of American households. Whereas I used to have three networks and less than a handful of local channels on the television at my beach house on Monterey Bay, I now have close to 200 channels with room to grow to 500, and some of them are already digital. My neighbor down the street chose satellite TV so he can get soccer games from around the world. Technology has given us the capability of demassifying media—not only in digital form, but also in print. Regional printing plants and satellite transmission have allowed the *Wall Street Journal* to print 14 regional editions daily, and the ads can be regionalized. I can now look for local real estate in the national newspaper on Fridays. Bank statements can be printed with personalized rewards. Tons of new magazines have sprung up around special interests of all sorts.

Why? Because the consumer is interested and because we can. This new, dazzling spectrum of choice is made possible with new data mining technology—the ability to sift through databases and efficiently find the people who are likely to be interested in a specific topic. I'm in the process of doing some remodeling, and in the magazine section of my local drugstore, in addition to the typical kitchen and bath remodeling magazines and home decorating publications, I found whole publications directed at log-home owners; those with Victorian houses; and mountain, beach, and island home owners; and many more. The same is true in the sports and health and fitness categories, which are now augmented to include not just diet and exercise, but alternative medicine.

We simply did not have this much information 20 years ago. We haven't yet even touched on the flow of information coming from the most exciting new technological innovation—the World Wide Web. The social, cultural, and marketing changes caused by the Web are simply staggering. Even more astounding is the fact that the Web has effectively been universally available only since the mid-1990s. This is such an important phenomenon that we'll talk about it in greater depth in its own chapter, because, in fact, it is one of the most important building blocks in the Knowledge Economy, and it is another factor enabling and driving companies to brand at ever greater speeds.

The combination of social changes of the last three decades, which has led to a more self-reliant and skeptical consumer, combined with the overabundance of information made possible by the technological revolution, has shifted far more of the brand power from the manufacturer to the consumer. True, all good brands have always been crafted with consumer relevance in mind, but think for just a minute about their focus, as captured in their ad campaigns. Volkswagen—"Think Small" or "Lemon." Avis—"We're number two, we try harder." "Don't squeeze the Charmin." "Two, two, two mints in one." Don't they all seem much more product focused than the brand messages of the 1990s? In the past, the brand became the voice of the manufacturer or service provider.

Contrast those with some of the powerful brand messages of today: "Just Do It," and "I Can" (by Nike). "Where do you want to

Volkswagen's "Lemon" ad.

Lemon.

This Volkswagen missed the boat.

The chrome strip on the glove compartment is blemished and must be replaced. Chances are you wouldn't have noticed it; Inspector Kurt Kroner did.

There are 3,389 men at our Wolfsburg factory with only one job: to inspect Volkswagens at each stage of production. (3000 Volkswagens are produced daily; there are more inspectors than cars.)

Every shock absorber is tested (spot checking won't do), every windshield is scanned. VWs have been rejected for surface scratches barely visible to the eye.

Final inspection is really something! VW inspectors run each car off the line onto the Funktionsprüfstand (car test stand), tote up 189 check points, gun ahead to the automatic brake stand, and say "no" to one VW out of fifty.

This preoccupation with detail means the VW lasts longer and requires less maintenance, by and large, than other cars. (It also means a used VW depreciates less than any other car.)

We pluck the lemons; you get the plums.

go today?" (by Microsoft). "The power to be your best," and now "Think Different" (by Apple). "Do you Yahoo!?" (by Yahoo!). All are significantly more personal.

The Gap, a very successful retail chain of clothing stores, is not about a tag line or campaign slogan, but an attitude. These relatively new brands have a much larger consumer component in their expression, and they have been built with significant consumer involvement. A good example is Doc Martens boots—they speak not to the manufacturer's capability, nor to the relative competitive positioning; rather, they speak directly to how the consumer thinks and feels using the product. This is an essential shift in thinking when addressing an informed consumer who is jaded about product claims and who is more likely to take his cues from informed friends than from an ad.

Technology marketers have known this for years. In every company and on every block in America, there is a techno-savvy consumer who becomes the de facto guru when buying technology. Sure, *PC Magazine* editorial ratings are considered, store personnel are queried, advertising is looked at; however, in the final analysis, it's the friend who knows a lot about this stuff who becomes the trusted source for decision making. That's why technology marketers have for so long emphasized the importance of decision influencers in their marketing programs. The last time I went into Fry's, the biggest electronics gadget store in our area, to buy a personal digital assistant, I ended up listening to three strangers—all young males—in the aisle who got into their own heated debate over what I should buy. I certainly wasn't impressed with the salesperson, who knew significantly less than these techno enthusiasts. It's exactly this kind of dynamic that helped the Palm computer become almost a cult product, selling a million units in its first year.

Even Procter & Gamble is taking the hint. In 1997, the Cincinnati-based packaged-goods giant announced that it was revamping its sales and marketing to let the consumer drive the supply chain rather than the other way around. A novel idea in the vast world of mass-marketed detergents and soaps, but day-to-day business in the technology industry in which you can get a built-to-order computer shipped within 24 hours. Procter & Gamble has responded to this shift in consumer direction by trying to determine which of its products are essential to the consumer and which are not. It is no longer trying to solve its own need for growth by foisting hundreds of brand extensions—slight reformulations under new names and repackagings of old stuff—on the supply chain with a demand that the product sell-through meet volume requirements for the brand.

New management at the company has cut back the entire P&G product lineup by almost 25 percent, and P&G is on track to slash another 20 percent by 2001. Unless a product can make the top two-thirds of a division's sales, it is history. The consumers will vote with their pocketbooks, and this time the vote will count.

This fundamental shift of brand power from the manufacturer to the consumer is happening because of the confluence of the new consumer, who is affected by technology and technology itself. Better sales data and more up-to-date tracking of product performance are possible, because technology lets companies learn instantly about the tastes, desires, and preferences of their customers. Probably the biggest technology advance in retailing has been the combination of handheld scanners with bar coding technology linked to sales and inventory databases. These portable devices are linking the selling floor with the back-office power of computer networks. Daily reports are available for analysis by the store and distributor—if there is one. Originally used to record revenue by SKU and manage inventory, these powerful systems now provide a wealth of information about customer choice. Interestingly, that information today is in the hands of the retailer—not the manufacturer.

The largest supermarket chain in North America, the Kroger Company, is taking this technology a step further. By teaming with Optimal Robotics and PSC Inc., Kroger has installed U-Scan Express self-checkout systems. The stations permit customers to scan, bag, and pay for their purchases all on their own. Customers can pay with cash, debit cards, or credit cards. This not only eliminates the need for help from store personnel, reducing store costs, it also fits well with the do-it-yourself mentality of American shoppers. Now the supermarket has established a brand relationship with the consumer, paving the way for store brands based on the market intelligence the store has collected.

How to Share the Brand with the Consumer–Lessons from Technology

So what can manufacturers do to put themselves closer to the customer—to cement a brand relationship that intermediaries cannot dissemble? There are plenty of examples of new brands that have done just that. Just look at Dell Computers. With more than $18 billion in sales in FY 1999, the company is racking up growth numbers that make your eyes spin. Sales have more than tripled, and profits are up fivefold in three years. Of all the Fortune 500 companies, only Dell has managed to increase sales and earnings more than 40 percent a year for each of the past three years (see Table 2.1).

Give them what they want. How does the company do it? By giving the customers exactly what they want, in time frames that are astonishing. In a word, Dell delivers. The Christmas of 1997, the company was able to ship 2,000 PCs and 4,000 servers, all loaded with appropriate software packages, to Wal-Mart stores on a just-in-time basis so there was no inventory lag. The October before, it delivered 8 large servers to the NASDAQ stock exchange in 36 hours!

Table 2.1 **The Explosive Growth of Dell Computer**

	FY95	FY96	FY97	FY98	FY99
Revenue ($B)	$3.5	$5.3	$7.8	$12.3	$18.2
Net Profit ($M)	$149	$272	$518	$944	$1,460

Think about it. Dell has no finished goods inventory. It's state of the art—all their machines come with the new Intel Pentium II chip. Dell learns directly from the market what the market wants. There are no middlemen, no intermediaries. If Dell detects that customers are beginning to request a specific configuration of a machine, it can plan ahead for more orders. Finally, because Dell gets paid by the people really using their machines, the company's receivables have a sterling credit rating. Customers pay just like traditional catalog shoppers, and Dell has the credit before the machine is even made. This push to get cozier with the customer is only getting stronger. Venturing overseas, Dell has direct sales relationships with large corporations, and has expanded its Internet operation to the point where it is selling more than $5 million a week on-line in Europe alone. Clearly, being able to configure machines to specific customer requests is key to satisfying the instant needs of corporate and individual customers.

Even more interesting is how Dell built a brand name for itself in an industry that is widely regarded as a commodity business. The pieces that go into making a computer are interchangeable. Open a Dell computer, and except for some minor configuration changes, you would be hard-pressed to distinguish it from a Compaq or a Gateway 2000 machine.

Brand a company capability rather than a fleeting product. What makes Dell different in the minds of the customers is less the product, and more the capability of the company. The ability to deliver exactly what the customer wants, whenever the customer wants it, and at a competitive price is critical to achieving a sales advantage. Dell's brand was built less on advertising and more on customer experience. With a stock market valuation of over $80 billion, Dell makes its mark in the customers' minds before they see or touch the machine. Dell's brand makes it comfortable for the customer to order a machine costing thousands of dollars by phone or via the computer—never having touched the product before it arrives. Dell makes its customers feel as if they are in control of the entire process, even allowing them to design their own configuration.

Get a one-to-one relationship going. More and more companies are becoming aware of the value of establishing a direct relationship with the consumer, jettisoning what were once independent resellers. Here again, technology companies have been setting trends and have managed to garner increasing profits along the way. By mid-1998, Dell and Gateway—the two largest direct-sales PC companies—had reached almost a 25 percent combined share of the U.S. PC market, double their 1996 share. Technology companies have always been good at getting close to the customer, probably because they had to. Technology companies have been notorious for shipping products that weren't quite finished, didn't quite work, or were so complex that the user had to be on the help line half of every day. As a result, tech companies began to develop the infrastructure for customer support. Things like FAQs (frequently asked questions) are commonplace and easily answered in technical manuals, on web sites, and under the Help button on your computer.

On-line help is increasingly available. Databases rich with customer information are being mined for marketing and product development purposes. When a packaged good is bought, the transaction ends; in technology, however, when a product is bought, the transaction begins. Software companies have perfected this to a black art, with release 1.2, 1.4, 2.0, and so forth. The initial purchase is simply the down payment on a stream of purchases, which the developers hope will last a lifetime.

Companies in all industries had better pay attention to getting close to the customer, or they will end up like Barnes & Noble, playing catch-up to a come-from-nowhere start-up called Amazon.com. Both companies actually have comparable market values, although Amazon.com has no stores, no retail real estate, no checkout lines, and no broken cash registers. It's too early to tell whether selling books on-line is a profitable business, but Amazon.com is clearly rewriting what it means to be a bookstore. Jeff Bezos, the founder and an industry outsider, has taken on the entrenched book-selling industry. By delivering on the promise of the "Earth's Biggest Bookstore," Amazon.com has become a formidable competitor to Barnes & Noble, even though Barnes & Noble has more than 1,000 store locations. Amazon.com has become a brand so powerful in two short years that it has caused Barnes & Noble to respond with a huge Internet effort of its own, including spending tens of millions of dollars to get a prime position on America Online.

Branding has helped define Amazon.com as more than just a convenient on-line service. It has extended its relationship with the customer through great personal service, all provided by the computer. One of my associates tells about the experience of ordering books from Amazon.com for the first time. He said it really felt like there was a caring, communicating human being plugged into the end of the Internet connection, not a computer. The computer (or is it really a person?) listened to his input, asked questions in plain English, seemed to anticipate his next move, and provided a near-human ordering experience—right down to an e-mail confirmation almost the instant the sale was completed. As you can imagine, he's a very satisfied Amazon.com customer. If you order a book by a certain author, you might just get an e-mail telling you that a new book has come in by the same author and asking you if you are interested in buying another book. That used to be the value point of the small independent bookstore until the chains put them out of business.

Go to Amazon.com and you'll find reviews of books written not just by professional reviewers, but by customers—the new and more believable "experts," who are given an incentive to be part of the Amazon.com community. By using technology to connect to its customers, Amazon.com has changed the sales equation. Buying a book is no longer a transaction, it is a relationship that extends beyond the 2.5 million titles in its inventory. The brand becomes less like a bookstore, and more of a community to connect with people who share similar interests. Best of all, the consumer feels empowered to browse the store and place orders at a private pace. Now, Amazon.com is working on extending the brand to the selling of music CDs, among other things.

Through the tools that technology provides, you as the brand builder have a whole new way to connect with your customer, literally and emotionally. You can now create a dynamic brand that can respond rapidly to the change that is so inevitable in our society. Product, service, and delivery can all be reorchestrated almost instantaneously. Whole on-line campaigns can be launched in days rather than months, responding to changing market conditions or special events.

Build partnerships to build brand quickly. Technology allows you to explore partnerships and alliances in ways that are difficult for traditional marketers. Amazon.com is able to initiate and implement its Associates Program with other technology leaders such as America Online, Yahoo!, Netscape, and the @Home Network. Through these partnerships, consumers are invited into the world of Amazon.com, almost like a referral from a friend. Even these kinds of relationships among brands, commonplace in technology, create different dynamics from a brand that is a stand-alone and that is tightly controlled by the manufacturer. Yet, while diffusing the brand and comingling it with other brands, these relationships create a stronger, interrelated brand network for the consumer.

How did technology marketers uncover this new kind of complex brand system? They stumbled on it. If you think about it, just about every technology product is a complex system made up of subsystems, each of which is developed and manufactured by a different industry. Take the computer, for example. Its components involve the semiconductor industry, disk drive industry, peripherals, power suppliers, monitors, and software industry, just to mention a few.

Branding issues get more complicated for the computer manufacturer when Intel spends $500 million a year on the now famous

"Intel Inside" campaign. When we launched Sony's PC based on Intel processors, Sony refused to put the Intel logo on its ads and forfeited the substantial financial contribution to its advertising, thinking that sharing with Intel would diminish the Sony brand. Their thinking was counter to the prevailing trend in the computer industry in which it has been proven that brands can coexist in harmony and end up supporting each other. Eventually, Sony succumbed and joined the "Intel Inside" program. In some sense, computer companies can be looked upon as virtual companies that are assembling an array of state-of-the-art technology and components from other companies—a far cry from the vertically integrated industrial giants of the past 50 years.

The technology industry has also pioneered with industry consortia [for example, the new Home Phoneline Networking Alliance, a consortium of 11 leading computing and communications companies (including Intel, Compaq, and AT&T), and Secure Electronic Transactions (SET) with Visa, MasterCard, American Express, IBM, and others]. Again, this was a necessary element of survival, as almost all products need to eventually connect. If they need to connect, there has to be a standard, and the standard has to be agreed upon by the myriad of players, and ultimately approved by the customer voting with their dollars. These consortia also impact the brand, which belongs to what I have come to call "the Brand Ecosystem™." This is an important concept, which I will explore further in Chapter 7.

This kind of intermixing of brands to surround the consumer with many friends is endemic to technology marketers, and now we are beginning to see the same process slowly infiltrate other industries. Hertz and American Express, for example, team up to offer double-class Hertz rental upgrades to small-business American Express cardholders. Lexus cars are choosing to cobrand with Coach leather bags.

In the entertainment industry, product placements in TV shows started out as just that. Now they have evolved into a whole

"Intel Inside"–a $500-million-per-year branding program.

Cobranding, American Express and Hertz.

This deal is priceless.

Hertz rents Fords and other fine cars.
® REG. U.S. PAT. OFF. © HERTZ SYSTEM INC.. 1999/025-98.

**Free double upgrade from Hertz. Exclusively for
American Express® Small Business Corporate Cardmembers.**

Ⓣo put it simply, you can't put a price on comfort. So we didn't.
In addition to the ongoing savings you receive as a Small
Business Corporate Cardmember, you now get not one, but two
full class upgrades from Hertz. Absolutely free. Just mention
PC#900970 at the time of your reservation and book it with
your American Express Corporate Card for Small Business. For
complete details, terms and conditions call your travel agent or
Hertz at **1-800-654-9998,** and be sure to visit us at **hertz.com**. Free
double upgrade, another reason nobody does it exactly like Hertz.

**Small Business
Services**

exactly.

new form of cobranding. Jerry Seinfeld can script a show around Jujubes; however, he won't promote a fancy stereo, because the show is about nothing, and only those brands that fit and augment the Jerry Seinfeld brand will be allowed. Another example of commingling of brands in the entertainment sphere occur with increasing frequency. Characters from one television show now appear as guest characters on other shows. *Law and Order*, which I enjoy watching, did a joint episode with another TV show, *Homicide*, in the hopes that the compatibility of the brands will cause some cross-pollination of viewers.

The Brand as Anchor

As on-line transactions become more efficient than other forms of direct selling and more convenient than traditional retailing, as products become more intangible because of customization, and as distribution moves to electronic, the only thing customers will have to grab on to is the brand. The brand can serve as an anchor, which can be pulled up to let the consumer sail into new waters, and then can be dropped again to provide safety for the night. Brands have to be made durable enough to withstand this added pressure.

However you choose to build your brand, speed and constant change are determining factors. Such is the nature of the new approach to branding that our many technology companies have discovered. The new kind of branding that my technology clients developed over the last two decades is quickly becoming the standard for the rest of the economy. To stay competitive, you will need to reevaluate your own approaches.

3

The Six Myths of Branding

Technology has spread its little tentacles everywhere, and the forces that have shaped technology have begun to affect virtually every other industry in most of the industrial world. Fluid by design, technology is invading and restructuring the way whole industries operate. With 40 to 50 years of brand identity built into the modern consumer's psyche, products such as Procter & Gamble's Tide offered the ad agency and the marketing team the time and leisure to test and retest any small or subtle modifications. Careful analysis of consumer reaction, chain-of-command approval, and launch programs as calibrated as moon shots were the norm.

If product introductions for washing detergent or television sets were orchestrated in a linear kind of slow-march shuffle into the future, it's because the very tools used to create these campaigns were part of a traditional linear process. Most of all, it is because there was *the luxury of time*. The whole process of rolling out a

global product might have taken years, without fear of obsolescence. When large U.S. consumer companies engineered their
plan of attack, the world was expected to fall in line, and mostly it
did. That's ancient history.

Technology Marketers: At Odds with Marketing

Brand building in the technology world has grown up with an
entirely different set of assumptions stemming from the very
nature of innovation. To accommodate its inherent need to move
quickly, to thrive on ambiguity, and to be open to experimentation
with a range of approaches, technology companies ignored the
rules of brand building, as we know them.

In doing so, they have been continuously criticized. Traditional
marketers have called technology companies unsophisticated and
unfocused. Actually, in the halls of corporate America's marketing
departments and large advertising agencies, the feelings expressed
are often ones of disgust. There are complaints about how awful
the advertising looks. There is much talk about how the consumer
is completely forgotten in the equation. There are constant comments that marketing is a stepchild at engineering-driven companies and that the prevailing attitude is one of "build a better
mousetrap." Everything is so chaotically fast that there is no time
to craft a brand properly, say these critics. Finally, they complain
that people with no skills in marketing, and often little business
experience, are making major advertising and marketing decisions. All of these points of view are right, and they are wrong.

Are They All Wet?

Yes, things in this new high-tech world move fast. Yes, people inexperienced in marketing will be part of the decision making, just as

marketing people will be taking part in product design decisions, and manufacturing may be contributing to pricing decisions. This is the natural outcome of companies organized to get to market fast, in which work is integrated and decisions are collaborative.

Yes, the consumer is often left until last. This is also the natural outcome of new-age companies organized to respond to market change by creating a stream of innovations. It reflects the very nature of innovation, which demands imagination and creative breakthroughs, inspiration, and tinkering, as opposed to the research-based facts and knowledge about consumer behavior, which drives decision making in the more traditional model. Decisions in these high-tech companies are based less on consumers answering the question, "What do I want?" and more on, "What if?"

"What if?" is by nature ambiguous, not really rooted in need or reality. It's visionary people like Ted Hoff, the coinventor of the microprocesser; Bill Gates of Microsoft, developer of the now ubiquitous software operating system adopted by the IBM PC; and Marc Andreesen and Jim Clarke of Netscape, who recognized what an Internet browser could do, who have produced real breakthrough products that changed the way we work and think. Their "what ifs" created new companies, new industries, and billions of dollars of valuation, and they have already impacted business, society, and global culture.

Yes, in an innovation-driven company, whatever group is responsible for the innovation will be its driving force. At Sony, it is the design team in Tokyo, the "digital dream kids," as Sony's Chairman Nobuko Idei likes to call them. At Apple and Intel, it is the engineers. At any fashion house, it will be the designer like Donna Karan or Calvin Klein. Contrast these forces creating innovation in high-tech industries with what's happening in the HMO industry today, for example, in which the driving force tends to be either an interest in community service, or regulatory pressure from government, and you get a sense of how different the determining force may be. Most HMOs have not figured out yet how to take control of their destiny and bring the driving force inside; as a result, they are playing catch-up. In the meantime, their margins are disappearing and the public and the press vilify them at every opportunity. In a get-it-now, the-way-I-want-it world, HMOs are looked at as an anachronism—packaged in bureaucracy.

Yes, the advertising for technology companies has not always been that memorable. The reason why high-tech has lagged

Early engineer-to-engineer ad.

386/AT CHIP SET COMPARISON

	G-2	C&T
CHIP COUNT	3	7
PROCESSOR SPEED	25 MHz	20 MHz
ADDITIONAL CHIPS NEEDED FOR FULL SYSTEM	14	33
MAXIMUM MEMORY	24 MB	16 MB

REGISTER PROGRAMMABLE CONFIGURATION OPTIONS

MEMORY MANAGEMENT	106	NOT EVEN CLOSE
HARDWARE OPTIONS	28	NOT EVEN CLOSE
I/O CONFIGURATIONS	30	NOT EVEN CLOSE
CLOCK OPTIONS	26	NOT EVEN CLOSE

We have one more number for you.
(408) 943-0224.

behind other sectors in the power of its promotional communications reaches back to the 1970s, when the marketing conversations of technology were almost exclusively engineer to engineer.

We were still developing revolutionary ideas like computers, databases, and cellular technology. The high-tech industry was focused on creating the enabling technologies that would eventually lead to killer products and applications. With deep-tech products to talk about, there were no mainstream advertising agencies equipped to translate this engineer speak into high-concept advertising. When a CEO comes to you and says that by using his new ASIC (Application Specific Integrated Circuit) chip, his customers can make a thousand new workstations with more computing power and more cheaply than their competitors, how many creative people sit up and say, "Wow—I can't wait to sell people on that message?" These people were truly technology pioneers in the days before technology became chic. These people were orphans and they proved to be wonderful clients for us in those early days.

Then, as the enabling technologies became more readily accessible in the 1980s, the focus of marketing conversations tended to shift to the engineer talking to the business buyer. Companies began to invest millions in information technology (IT) at an ever-increasing pace. A strategic new position was developed and entered the ranks of senior corporate management—the chief information officer (CIO), who more recently has given growth to another specialty—the chief knowledge officer (CKO). The industry was focused on building infrastructure. Most of the advertising in the technology field was clearly business to business, but still with engineering trying to explain to the chief technologist of the customer why this particular mousetrap was better. As the industry evolved, by the middle to late 1980s, professional marketers began to take over the conversations and, as the investment in technology began to stretch into the billions, the advertising began to move into general business books and occasionally onto

television. Finally, general advertising agencies began to take high tech seriously and made an investment in people who had some familiarity with it.

The early agency leaders still tended to be clustered around Silicon Valley—names like Hodskins, Simone and Searle (which was recently acquired by Publicis), Tycer Fultz Bellack (which was acquired by BBDO and disappeared), Winkler Advertising, Anderson Lembke (one of Microsoft's two lead agencies today), and Saatchi & Saatchi all helped build great high-tech brands working out of offices around San Francisco and San Jose. Further afield, what is now TBWA/Chiat/Day and BBDO/West proved effective at building Apple; Lord Einstein Frederico, and more recently Ogilvy & Mather Worldwide in New York, took on building the IBM brand around the world. Intel turned to a Salt Lake City–based agency, EuroRSCG Dahlin Smith White; Compaq relied on Ammirati Puris Lintas in New York, and more recently DDB Needham, to build its brand. All of these first-rate agencies shared one attribute in common: They knew how to celebrate the mainstreaming of technology.

As the technologies on which business began to depend—computers, modems, color printers, graphics software, fax machines, cell phones, on-line services—became even cheaper, we saw consumers begin to buy. Now, with the sub-$1,000 PC, the $200 printer, and the free cell phone, price is no longer a deterrent. As the products became easier to use, technology graduated from being regarded as a niche category to being considered a major advertising category.

Now the question arises, How should agencies and clients define the target audience for high-tech products for the mass business market? Saying you want adults "25 to 49" doesn't work. Kids buy pagers and cell phones with their own money. Grandparents buy computers and subscribe to America Online to communicate with their grandkids. An example of mainstream technology is the Motorola Wings TV. With high-tech companies spending an esti-

Motorola Wings TV: technology goes mainstream.

mated $5 billion, no one can say anymore that technology adver-
tising is niche or second-class. The media spend has even fueled
some wonderful advertising—which is beginning to win gold at
major international advertising competitions like Clio and
Cannes. Just look at the AT&T ad for the mom taking a "meeting" at the beach, and her young daughter asking, "When can I be
a client?" or the recent Apple "Think Different" work from
TBWA/Chiat/Day—including a TV ad that won an Emmy and
the print campaign that won a gold at the Clios. These are wonderful commercials, no matter what category.

Over the past 15 years, I've had the opportunity to observe 50 or
more technology companies with which we have worked—from little start-ups (like LSI Logic, who became the world leader in ASIC
chips and is still our client, and Ascend Communications with their
firm foothold in networking equipment) to large multinationals
(like 3Com, Sony, and Hewlett-Packard). We have watched the
traditional myths of brand building being deconstructed. Add to
that the years of experience our staff has accumulated before joining
the agency—working for blue-ribbon brands like Apple, IBM, Intel,

Apple's "Think different" ad.

Compaq, and Microsoft—we can say, unblushingly, that we represent the new culture of knowledge economy marketing.

It has not always been pretty, nor always graceful. However, things usually aren't when they are brand new. Even the new principles of branding have required a little debugging over time. Let's examine the myths to see where we stand.

The Six Myths of Branding

THE MYTH . . .	THE NEW REALITY
1. A brand is built over a long time.	A brand can be built at warp speed.
2. A brand is precisely crafted for a tightly defined target.	A brand is expansive.
3. Advertising is the major creator of a brand.	Advertising is only one arrow in the quiver.
4. Brand the product.	Brand a bigger idea.
5. The brand needs a manager.	The brand needs a shepherd.
6. The brand is a marketing concept.	The brand is a financial concept.

Myth 1: A Brand Is Built over a Long Time

It is written in stone that it takes a long time—years, in fact—to establish a brand in the national psyche. I've even included this truth in lectures to business schools around the country. What is *time?* Ivory Soap is 125 years old; Tide, 50; Crest, 40. Apple is only a little more than 20 years old, a mere child in the brand sandbox, but it certainly has developed a fanatical following. The important thing, however, is that Steve Jobs and company accomplished that feat within Apple's first few years, when they introduced the Macintosh computer in 1984. America Online, with awareness in American households as high as 80 percent, and Yahoo! are still very young companies, strong as they already are, and their brands were built in a handful of years. Then, of course, there are Amazon.com, and the Palm computer, both of which became sensations almost overnight.

With the advent of new communications technologies, it is now possible to spread the word, like a village drumbeat, to all corners of the world in months, weeks, or even days. The drumbeat is often carried by the users themselves—a more believable source of information in our jaded, skeptical society. Satjiv Chahil, one of Sony's marketing people and a highly respected member of the digital community, put out an electronic drumbeat for the new Sony sub-notebook. Prior to the introduction or even the availability (a common practice in technology is a preannouncement months before the product is available) of the notebook, he used his personal Rolodex to send personalized e-mails to the Who's Who of technology influencers. He then gave them a chance to have a PC first, at a special price, all because they were in the know and they were friends. I was fortunate enough to get one of those e-mails, and like almost everyone else who got one, I responded with an immediate yes. The result? A substantial number of direct orders were delivered very early in the cycle, and the "right people"—the digital influencers, flying around on airplanes with the cute little purple metal notebook—created a buzz everywhere they went.

Amazon.com, founded in 1995, became the leading web commerce site, and arguably the best-known web brand, in the space of two years. Word of mouth, public relations and publicity, programs to influence the opinion leaders, and a highly positive I-know-what-this-brand-is-all-about experience with the web site itself, all combined to build a brand initially before any paid advertising.

A brand is built over a long time.

A brand can be built at warp speed.

The Myth #1

The New Reality

America Online began to build its brand by using the technique of mass giveaway. I recall sitting on my RenoAir flight and received a diskette with my snack. They also put diskettes into Rice Chex boxes and polybagged them with magazines. As a result, they went from less than a million subscribers to over 16 million in a handful of their early years, and today can promise the biggest single paid audience of any service on the Web.

Netscape, on the other hand, built an entire company in less than two years also on the concept of the giveaway. Their browser became the de facto standard by being distributed free on the Internet, while they made their money on the server side. Only when Microsoft began a similar program, going a step further and embedding its browser in the operating systems of its Windows software, did Netscape begin to understand that, although its company was a digital household name, it hadn't really created a brand yet.

The Palm computer, the handheld electronic organizer developed by US Robotics and then acquired by 3Com in Silicon Valley, took little more than a year to sell its first million units. It was able to do so both with an aggressive advertising campaign and an "influence the influencers" program. By demonstrating the product at select industry conferences and offering the product at half price to opinion leaders, the enthusiasts became a sales force by example. No paid sales force could have done as well as quickly at any price. Now, in less than three years, we are on version 5 of the Palm computer itself. Last week, I received in the mail an entire catalog from other companies offering accessories and software to go along with it. The Palm computer has developed a very loyal, almost cultish, following and a strong relationship with its customer. It is unquestionably a valuable brand—built in almost no time at all.

Apple itself, it can be argued, was launched with a single high-impact creative event. The now famous "1984" commercial with the blond woman runner throwing a hammer at a screen ran only once as paid media, on the Super Bowl. The PR that this exciting and controversial spot garnered, and the consequent rerunning of the commercial by commentators for free, was phenomenally successful in building excitement for launch of the Mac. In typical Jobsian fashion, Apple didn't rely only on the commercial. It blanketed every seat of the Super Bowl stadium with Apple seat covers, so that all of America could see the logo in the pregame coverage and it made sure that certain treasured members of the trade press were present when Jobs previewed the commercial at a sales meeting.

Therefore, yes, brands are built over time, but time for high-tech products can be measured in nanoseconds. Marketers are now as impatient as our young consumers. Even venture capitalists, who 10 years ago funded only development talent and technology, now fund branding campaigns. They know that building excitement for the brand is directly related to the value of the company—hence, higher valuations at the IPO, the magic "exit strategy" of the venture capitalist. If building the brand can be done now, as proven by successful companies, then why wait?

Myth 2: A Brand Is Precisely Crafted for a Tightly Defined Target

Think back to brand briefs some years ago, or even to the way companies used to use MRI and Neilsen audience-tracking data. The brand's target was defined demographically—"women 21 to 34 with one or more children, in households with $25,000+ annual income"—a simple definition reflecting a simpler world. Then, what was called psychographics began to find its way into the brand audience definition, expanding beyond simple demographics to add such descriptors as "upwardly mobile" or "empty nesters." This was a way of noting that people were more individualistic, even though their life patterns were very similar.

Although the brand definition, "women 21 to 34" sounds exceptionally broad to us today, it didn't when this practice was developed. Going back to our earlier discussions of society and culture, we were a more unified society and culture then, with value systems and social rules that people generally accepted and followed. Life patterns were more predictable: get married in your early twenties, have kids, work, retire, and die. Concepts such as life-long learning, multiple careers, households other than the nuclear family were generally unknown. Houses didn't sport *two* master bedrooms, and they weren't built following the principles of Feng Shui—why in the world would you need that?

Information flow was narrower. The TV networks and print media reinforced social and cultural expectations for Americans who were by and large isolated from the rest of the world—America becoming the world's most populous island. In the manufacturer's world, building the brand was a simple proposition, too. Companies tended to be vertically integrated, and every step of the branding process was easily under their control. In those not-so-long-ago days, it was pretty easy to focus on one stakeholder, the narrowly defined target customer, and make the brand strategy work.

A brand is precisely crafted for a tightly defined target.

The Myth #2

A brand is expansive.

The New Reality

Today, things are very different. The speed of change, the abundance of available information and the new ways it gets disseminated, as well as different ways of organizing corporate work, have made it necessary to view stakeholders in a brand differently. Today's brand must be crafted with its future in mind. Remember, everything is changing. For example, Apple's "the power to be your best" brand strategy, although extremely powerful with individuals, was probably one of the contributing factors to its singular lack of success in the corporate sector.

The brand must be more expansive, not just in terms of time, but also in terms of stakeholders. It has to not only embrace a more splintered society, it must also accommodate the much more complicated group of stakeholder relationships caused by the virtual corporation. Today's brands exist in a complex, fluid amalgam that encompasses the manufacturer, the distributor, the consumer, alliances, partnerships and joint ventures, employees, investors, and analysts. The simple structure of "one brand, one brand audience" has been replaced by a constantly changing, flexible, sometimes multibranded environment in which a brand must be broad enough to touch all its constituencies, yet simple enough to be understandable to all. Rich enough to stretch, yet specific enough to be personal.

The questions that consumers and brand builders alike must answer seem bewildering at times. If I buy a new cell phone, am I buying AirTouch cellular service, the Motorola StarTac phone, or even the service and postsale support of Quality Cellular? When I buy a new PC, do I care most about whether it's a Compaq, Dell, HP, Sony, or IBM product—or am I more concerned that it contains an Intel microprocessor instead of AMD or Cyrix? When I'm launching a new company, am I more interested in carving out a clear company brand positioning in the minds of my customers, or for the market and financial analyst community, or for those behind-the-scenes influencers who can make or break me?

The answer is, in fact, "All of the above." Now the brand begins to look more like our new consumer and to behave more like our new-age company. Brands are becoming more collaborative and fluid, more intangible, and more emotional because they need to transcend their physical attributes to survive.

Myth 3: Advertising Is the Major Creator of a Brand

In the world of mass manufacturing, mass marketing, and mass distribution, this was absolutely true. P&G, Colgate, GM, Ford, and Chrysler spent vast amounts on advertising because it was the key way to assure brand contact with their consumers and, in many cases, with lots of middlemen in the distribution chain. Without the information technologies we take for granted today, advertising really created the brand, and other elements of marketing played a significantly less important role.

In today's world, the brand is created in many additional ways. How did we get here? Mostly, it is because technology has allowed

Advertising is the major
creator of the brand.

Advertising is only one arrow in the quiver.

The Myth #3

The New Reality

the manufacturer to find the specific individual consumer and deliver the brand promise directly. Thank you databases, data mining, automatic computer dialing, and of course, e-mail, just to name a few.

Technology has enabled marketers to create a buzz about a brand and get it noticed in an unbelievably short time. In 1996, Kinetix®, a San Francisco multimedia company owned by Autodesk, developed an animation software package. Part of the demo package was a funky dancing baby character. Somehow, the Dancing Baby™ got sent as an attachment in an e-mail, and made such a hit that it started getting passed around, usually with music added, from friend to friend, all over the world. In a handful of months, the Dancing Baby began appearing on web sites almost like a cult icon. The *New York Times* ran a story on it, and the Baby hit prime time in a January 1998 episode of the hit show *Ally McBeal*. *Ally McBeal* won two Golden Globes, the Baby clip was shown, and Kinetix was launched into the big time.

Kinetix Dancing Baby character.

(*Source:* "Images courtesy of Kinetix®, a division of Autodesk®, Inc. © Copyright 1996–99, Autodesk, Inc./Unreal Pictures Inc.)

Public relations has also taken on a whole new role in brand building today. Technology companies have grown up knowing that. They are masters of influencing the influencers. Again, this is a natural outcome of technology. It's not difficult to understand why. You want someone you trust to make a recommendation; therefore, you turn to your "geek in the know." How does your geek become familiar with brands he or she has never yet touched or tried? They find out from influential gurus they trust, like Esther Dyson and Dick Shaffer, who put on conferences and send out newsletters at several hundred dollars a pop, keeping up the image of exclusivity and being in the know.

MC, a well-read monthly about high-tech marketing, puts out an annual ranking of the hottest media (the *Wall Street Journal* is No. 1), the top influencers (Walter Mossberg, a columnist for the *Wall Street Journal*, is No. 1), and top journalists (top spots go to

Jesse Berst, editorial director of ZDNet Anchor West, for the Web; Spencer Katt, columnist for *PC Week,* for gossip; Eric Lundquist, editor-in-chief of *PC Week,* for the trades; and Stewart Alsop, columnist for *Fortune,* for pundits). These are the kinds of people that technology companies work hard to court and to impress. It's all part of the influence-the-influencers approach to building a brand that technology companies understand so well.

This technique of influencing the influencer, heavily used by technology companies, is now finding its way into the marketing of ordinary consumer companies. The technique works well with the skeptical consumer in an information-rich society. Hennessy, a brand of cognac, hired young good-looking people to sit at bars all over the country ordering a Hennessy martini drink, creating conversation about it—the buzz. It made the Hennessy brand cool—by creating a group of influencers.

In 1998, Daewoo Motor Co., the Korean car giant, recruited 2,000 Daewoo campus advisors. They are young, enthusiastic students hired to create a buzz about a new car. These Daewoo campus advisors will be talking up the cars as they drive them around campus for free. They'll be holding Daewoo events, and collecting a commission of $300 to $500 for each car sold.

Technology companies, however, gravitated to PR as a brand-building tool because it was fast, it influenced the opinion leaders, and it was less costly than advertising. Public relations takes advantage of the value of the media as a news and information dissemination vehicle, with greater credibility than paid advertising, to create and nurture brand positioning. Some PR firms even evaluate their success on the basis of the "equivalent advertising value" of the brand's PR coverage, based on column inches or television minutes, and the ratio can be staggering—the value of an impression can run 10 or 20 times the actual cost of PR against advertising.

Technology Solutions, Inc. in New York, the public relations agency for IBM, came up with the Deeper Blue computer–versus–

Gary Kasparov chess match in 1996, a PR coup that captured the world's imagination.

The rematch in 1997 was a carefully orchestrated media event, which included things like personality marketing to infuse the Deeper Blue computer with the personalities of the system's designer and IBM research consultants from the chess world; creating a media sports center for the match, designed to provide the press with human interest, "color comment," and move-by-move coverage; and close cooperation with IBM's Internet Division to create on-line opportunities for media outreach, ticketing, and on-line match news tracking. The program resulted in a campaign that reached over 3 billion readers, listeners, and watchers worldwide. The IBM Deeper Blue web site received over 74 million hits during the nine-day match, and IBM stock reached an all-time high of 177⅛ during the course of the match, attributed by the media, *USA Today*, and the *Wall Street Journal* to the Deeper Blue match.

Fresh Express Farms (a leader in packaged salads), handled by the San Francisco public relations firm, Fineman Associates, had results as strong for their client. Using a series of PR tactics, Fineman PR secured some 330 story placements about Fresh Express and two appearances on the *Today Show* in the space of nine months in 1995. This positive PR coverage helped achieve an increase in annual sales over that period of time from $189 million to over $300 million.

Another vehicle for brand building in which technology companies excel is customer service. Their help lines are always busy. Customer service can help you configure your computer. In-house telemarketing people, whose databases are linked to the help line and customer-support database, can suggest another piece of software you could use based on past conversations with you. How you are treated at each of these interactions is a vital part of the brand.

Take United Airlines, for example. Want to check your frequent flier miles account at 11:30 P.M. on a Sunday? No problem.

Want to order that special kosher meal for your next flight? Just click here. In this example, UAL is able to combine the process of selling a service with the collection of data in a seamless set of keystrokes. By doing it so well, it is enhancing the brand with every one of those keystrokes.

This is just a first step. To access the United System via its web site, the user must enter a host of personal data about his or her flying preferences. So, say good-bye to all those expensive focus groups in which people—usually down on the ground—answer questions about air travel. Now, passengers can tell United exactly what it needs to know to provide better service and a better product. The Internet site that lets customers literally get a window seat represents a sea change in the way producers of products and services are connecting with their customers. This will continue to grow as consumers get more comfortable with the experience. The technology that permits companies to communicate and share data in vast quantities internally is now approaching the level of sophistication and simplicity that offers all individuals the same opportunities.

Transacting business on-line with an airline appears natural now, but many worried it would change the relationship of the customer to the brand. They were right, but not the way they suspected. The response was overwhelmingly positive. Cathay Pacific Airlines hosted several on-line auctions for airplane tickets from the United States to Hong Kong in 1996. The event was so successful that the airline has repeated the effort with a "Cyber Traveler" promotion. These promotions connect travelers with offers in which they have already indicated an interest. The link between buyers and sellers is fostered on the basis of predisposed need rather than one-directional marketing. The happy result is that the brand becomes more personal, the relationship more lasting, and the financial value of the brand increases exponentially.

When mass manufacturing and mass marketing forces prevailed, advertising was a central component in building a brand.

In this era, network television dominated the media scene and delivered huge audiences—more by far than any other medium. The top-rated television shows like *Cosby* and *Bonanza* could achieve 35+ ratings, reaching nearly one out of three homes with a single TV commercial. Brands were built and sustained on the basis of advertising dollars and advertising impressions. The question clients wanted answered was: How many gross rating points are we delivering? "We'd better achieve at least 400 GRPs with an 85 reach and a 4.7 frequency to reach our audience effectively," was typical client speak.

In the traditional model, advertising was the key spending component of new brand introductions (with the exception of the huge cost of delivering initial product samples by mail or door-to-door to vast numbers of homes). I remember, as a young mother, coming home from work and finding a small bottle of Wisk hanging on my doorknob. It has been a long time, though, since I've seen another one. There are too many more efficient and less costly ways of delivering samples today. Now, I find them in little packages glued to the pages of magazines or in the rain wrap on my newspaper. America Online diskettes were delivered through various channels—even placed in cereal boxes. As for software, I can sample it by a quick click and a download from the Web. The software will come to me with a built-in expiration date. I can try before I buy—but eventually, I'll have to plunk down my money.

Another case history, and one of the most successful case histories of branding in technology, is the "ingredient-branding" story of Intel. Intel reportedly spent $500 million a year in advertising to promote a semiconductor chip inside the computer—a part the consumer didn't see, didn't know, or didn't care about. The program was called "Intel Inside." On the surface, it looked like a classic branding program supported by an unheard-of level of ad spending for the technology world.

Intel had a brilliant hidden strategy. Although Intel achieved very high worldwide name recognition, our research told us that, by itself, the Intel ads did little to build the brand. Consumers knew that Intel makes good chips and that's about all. In human terms, Intel became an "acquaintance," but not a "friend"—as one would expect of a high-profile brand.

The brilliance of the strategy lay in the "Intel Inside" *program*. If, as a computer manufacturer, you ordered enough Intel chips and put the "Intel Inside" logo on your ad, Intel would underwrite a significant portion of the media expense. This was, in effect, a disguised discount on the chips. The chip price stayed the same, keeping revenues and stock prices high, whereas a volume discount was applied to advertising. As a result, computer manufacturers began cobranding their computers with the Intel name, the logo got even wider recognition, and consumers began to perceive it as a benefit in performance and reliability of their purchase.

Advertising would stimulate demand for each of Intel's customers, and of course, Intel also benefited. Once the computer makers got hooked on the millions of dollars of advertising, like junkies, it was hard to kick the habit. Compaq tried, claiming Intel's brand diluted theirs, but eventually came back. It was just too good of a deal.

The impact of the program continues to this day. Intel went to every publisher and network and negotiated fabulous volume discounts for everyone who participated in the program. Publishers were excited because the program appeared to bring them many new advertisers and helped prove the value of advertising. The computer manufacturers got better rates through the program than they would have buying ratecard prices, and Intel substantially reduced the total cost for its own advertising while maintaining high exposure for "Intel Inside."

Cobranding is an interesting means for reducing the cost of building brands through advertising. If you can trade on an established brand name, the cost of creating *your* own brand can be less. The credit card industry, a relatively new technology industry, is full of such cobranding situations—combining Visa or MasterCard with any one of hundreds of financial or other retail organizations, and sharing database lists to appeal to each other's customers. Use your General Motors–affiliated MasterCard and accumulate credits for your next GM car or truck. Use your First Bank Visa and you'll receive frequent flier miles on United, or use your Citibank Visa for miles on American Airlines.

Today, everything you do shapes the brand. With the United States moving increasingly toward a service-dominated economy, even the personnel or technology performing the service contributes to the brand-building activity. A clean, efficient order taker is part of the brand of In-N-Out, a southern California hamburger chain that has expanded into northern California. The menu is short, the traffic high, and the operation highly mechanized, so no hamburger lays around for even a minute. The impression is that each hamburger is cooked to order. It's a fresh-tasting hamburger—the meat and the bun are hot; the lettuce and the tomato are cold. Whereas you see people lining up at In-N-Out, the McDonald's next door is empty. In-N-Out has advertised over time, but modestly. What they have relied on most is "the buzz"— happy customers sending their friends over for lunch, dinner, or a hamburger snack at all hours of the day.

Today, advertising dollars are not as important as they used to be. In fact, significant brands have been built with no advertising dollars at all. Amazon.com became a household word in the rapidly growing world of Internet users without spending a penny in traditional media, as did Netscape and Yahoo! They relied on word of mouth, on creating buzz in the market, and on the opinions of influential market gurus and analysts. They paid significant sums to link to sites on the Web, and they paid for banners. Perhaps most important, they relied on the actual experience of consumers who tried their product or service, and became loyal, repeat customers.

Myth 4: Brand the Product

Once upon a time, the prevailing wisdom was that the consumer relationship was based on the product alone, not the company that produced it. So, the logical extension to this thinking was that P&G wasn't an important brand in the consumer's mind; it was Downy and Crest that got all the attention. General Motors even went so far a few years ago as to stop emphasizing its five main car *divisions* in its advertising, such as Chevrolet and Buick; rather, it started considering each model the brand that mattered—such as Lumina or Skylark. The corporation regarded itself as merely a holding company with a portfolio of brands.

Technology companies, however, found that they could not operate this way. With product life cycles routinely as short as nine months and some creeping into the six-month range, it simply was not cost-effective to brand just the product. With brands being established at warp speed and with less dollar expenditure, it made sense to brand something that could carry the equity forward or possibly transfer it to another product. Just as fire was discovered by accident when someone rubbed two stones together, technology companies discovered a new way to think about a brand. Instead of branding a fleeting product, it might make more sense to brand the company, which would be around for a longer time, or perhaps a technology platform that could be carried for future products.

The revelation for high-tech advertisers came when they realized they could brand the idea behind their product, as well as the product itself. That's why more of the activity is being slanted toward "bigger ideas," such as "Intel Inside," "Powered by Cisco,"

Brand the product.   Brand a bigger idea.

The Myth #4   The New Reality

and Apple's "Think Different." Microsoft has done a great job of extending its operating system brand to a slew of applications software products, including "Microsoft Word," "Microsoft Works," "Microsoft Explorer," and hundreds of others. It's even moving into the media business with MSNBC, *Slate,* and web sites like Sidewalk and Expedia. Whatever Microsoft touches—and it's plenty—you know it has got Bill Gates' Big M thumbprint behind it.

Contrast this with Software Publishing, a since forgotten company, which acquired software titles and tried to use the standard packaged-goods branding approach to sell them. When the company became dependent on Harvard Graphics, a presentation software, as its major source of revenue, and Harvard Graphics fell behind in technology and lost ground to Aldus Persuasion, Software Publishing tried to move into other software areas. By then, however, the company had become synonymous with Harvard Graphics, and presentation software. Software Publishing by itself was nothing. The marketplace would not allow the company any maneuvering room. We saw this sad, but not uncommon, story replayed in the media again and again: The board removes the founder; the new management tries to restart the company; the stock tanks; the company sells off some remaining bits of intellectual property to someone else; and the stockholders have new wallpaper for their bathrooms.

Intel helped itself deal with technology churn by branding a technology platform. The whole x86 family, from 286 chips through 386 and 386SX to 486, became a brand that lasted a decade. Then all that equity was successfully transferred to the Pentium processor, which is likely to have an even longer life, if Intel continues to be smart.

Consider for a minute the mutual funds industry's story. The industry has seen remarkable growth in the past 10 years, fueled by phenomenal increases in IRA, 401(K) and similar retirement plan investments, and by the decline of traditional pension plans. The longest bull market in U.S. history hasn't hurt either. Baby boomers have been flocking to mutual funds as the issue of retirement began to enter their thoughts.

This push into mutual funds has caused a massive proliferation of new product lines. Today, there are hundreds of fund families and over 9,000 mutual funds, which use almost every conceivable investment approach: aggressive growth; balanced, growth, and income; small-cap, mid-cap, large-cap; index funds; European, Asian, and emerging markets; and more. Change in the industry, even turmoil, is constant with new funds, new directions, and new managers. Add to that mergers, acquisitions, and new debates about passive index funds versus actively managed funds, about investing based on company fundamentals versus overall market trends and momentum, and you get a sense of all the diverse forces driving this industry. Yet, in this confusing morass, some strong brands have emerged very quickly. Among the leaders are Vanguard, Fidelity, and Janus.

Now, let's look at Vanguard. First, it's a prime example of a powerful new brand that was based on a company, not an individual product. How is it possible to recoup the dollars spent behind a single product offering when it is likely to be obsolete within a couple of years or even months? The answer is don't brand the product; instead, brand the company, the platform, or the family or philosophy on which it's based, whatever is extendable. Sure, Vanguard may be best known for its indexed stock and bond funds, but the Vanguard brand goes beyond any particular fund to achieve an overarching brand promise as the *low-expense, long-term investment choice*, and the brand delivers. It is grounded in the bedrock of strong, long-term performance, some of the lowest fund expenses ratios in the country, and the clear vision of its senior management. This brand promise is communicated across all Vanguard marketing and investor communications programs. No loud hype, no boastful claims, just straight talk about an investor's objectives and investment time frame, the track record of appropriate Vanguard funds over the long term, and the considerable importance of low expenses over time. This message is delivered consistently—to the individual investor and by the CEO to major players in the financial community. It has worked. Vanguard has grown to some $400 billion in mutual fund assets, and it has established what is arguably the most powerful brand in the mutual fund industry.

Visa is also pursuing the single-brand approach with subbrands to distinguish new types of Visa-branded products and to extend Visa's brand equity to get the new products started on a strong footing. Visa has elected to introduce VisaCash and Visa Electron, unlike MasterCard, which is introducing Mondex for cash and Maestro for debit cards, a whole new set of brand names that don't carry the halo effect of the Master brand.

The lesson to be learned now, when looking to build a brand, is that it is important to look beyond the tangible product, which is more than likely to change over time, and think about what can be the sustaining deep core of the brand, the essence, which is virtually unchanging.

Myth 5: The Brand Needs a Manager

Yes, the brand manager can determine the brand promise, the brand character, and the brand personality. He or she can decide what is the optimum price, the best distribution, and how many cases should ship. The brand manager can direct the agency to get the kind of advertising that will best resonate with the target. It's the brand manager's responsibility to plan and execute the test market. Those are the kinds of decisions that were expected from a classically trained brand manager.

But wait! We've already agreed that things are different today. The brand is no longer being launched into an orderly world. Today, the marketplace has become a topsy-turvy, bouncing world—like the deck of an aircraft carrier in a Force 10 gale. The issue, therefore, is how do you launch in this turbulent new world? This brings us to our next "reality."

Factors such as globalization, partnerships, and alliances have complicated the life of a brand manager. These are brand-influencing factors that are essentially out of the brand manager's control.

If you look at the history of American brands, you will note that they were generally launched in the United States, became established, and then went overseas for expansion. Bits of phrases like "non-U.S.," "foreign markets," "expat," "copy translations," and "home office" pepper the language. When examined, it's apparent that each of these phrases reflects a very U.S.-centric focus. Technology companies, on the other hand, have historically launched globally almost immediately. It is typical in this industry for an early-stage company to have 45 to 55 percent of its early revenue from outside the United States.

It was in the mid-1980s when I remember meeting Wilf Corrigan, the founder and chairman of LSI Logic, a leading semiconductor manufacturer in Silicon Valley. Corrigan corrected me when I referred to an "international market." He instructed me that the correct word was "global." That was the first time I had heard "global" used in conjunction with business, and it felt strange on my tongue. Today, we've learned to think global, and the word represents a larger perspective.

In such a global marketplace, what exactly does a brand manager manage? Our historical approach of exporting U.S. brands overseas has been providing lots of entertainment on "Bloopers and Blunders" lists for many years. The very popular Ford Pinto had to readjust its marketing strategy in Brazil in the late 1970s when it realized that *pinto* was a Portuguese slang word for "tiny penis." The Chevy Nova meant "no go" in Spanish—not an ideal brand for an automobile. Parker pens advertised a ballpoint pen that promised "It won't leak in your pocket and embarrass you." The translation in Mexico, erroneously using the word *embarazar* for "embarrass," had ads running with "It won't leak in your pocket and make you pregnant." Frank Perdue's slogan, "It takes a tough man to make a chicken tender," showed up in Spanish as "It takes a virile man to make a chicken aroused."

With little firsthand knowledge of the changing marketplace and less and less control over where the brand will end up, *over what* does the brand manager in the new Knowledge Economy preside? The targets are all over the place, the messages aren't as crisp as one might like, and things are moving quickly.

To complicate the situation even further, technology companies have pioneered, in a big way, the concept of strategic alliance. This has taken many forms, from joint technology developments like Intel and HP on the merced chip, to comarketing arrangements like ZDNet and MSNBC, to ingredient branding like the Intel Inside program that we discussed previously or the Cisco Powered program (an Intel copycat but with less muscle). It reaches from industry consortia like Sematech, a consortium of

U.S. semiconductor companies; the Power PC consortium of IBM, Apple, and Motorola; and the Home Phoneline Networking Alliance (Home PNA), which includes heavyweights such as AT&T, Compaq, Hewlett-Packard, IBM, and Intel. There are outsourcing agreements (like Intel-manufactured Sony PCs), second-sourcing agreements (like Intel's early agreements with AMD to build 386 chips), and even whole new companies set up with equity participation by the infrastructure providers.

Globalstar, for example, a new satellite telephony company formed by Loral Space and Communications, is an example of this kind of business model. Loral owns about one-third and provides the satellites and satellite technology, working with other equipment and aerospace systems manufacturers who are both equity and strategic partners. Telecommunications service providers like AirTouch, France Telecom, and Vodafone will provide global service and are also equity partners. Qualcomm, the second-largest owner, will provide phones and will also manufacture ground control centers. In this model, the customer gets the whole service; the brand manager gets a headache. What should the branding system be? With at least three, and maybe four, brands each with their own strengths and weaknesses coming together to produce the service, whose brand should be allowed to rise to the top and create a lasting relationship with the customer? Brand is value. Who should pay for building that value? Who should get the ultimate benefit?

With all these different stakeholders, many elements swinging far out of the brand manager's control, constant ambiguity being added to the brand-building process, the brand manager ends up feeling like she or he is herding cats. Cats don't herd, but sheep do. For that reason, I prefer to call the brand manager "The Brand Shepherd." Keep the flock intact, keep the flock safe. Take it to new pastures when needed, and bring it home. The brand shepherd's primary role is to define the *core* of the brand—the most *universal* truth—not its

The brand needs a manager.

The Myth # 5

The brand needs a shepherd.

The New Reality

style or window dressing, which is likely to change with time, task, and geography. Then the brand shepherd must evangelize the brand strategy to all the constituents, all the stakeholders.

What is a brand? When I talk to people about what is a brand, especially people outside of the marketing world, like my husband's banker and lawyer friends, I find it helpful to use the analogy of a person. A person has character, personality, interests, and hobbies. A person goes through stages as he or she matures and as life events work their changes. In the 1960s, I wore Birkenstocks, burned my bra, and was a teaching assistant at San Jose State. In the 1980s, I wore Joan Collins power suits, did lunch, and drank only wine and designer water. Today, the office environment is dress down; I'm a little wiser (hopefully) and a little more philosophical. My character and fundamental value system, however, remain the same.

A brand can change its clothes, too (have different ad campaigns, packaging, and so forth), and it can do different things (make different products and services), but its core values and character should be virtually unchanging.

A brand, in its relationship with the consumer, must move from the acquaintance stage to the friendship stage to achieve its full power. Why? If you have only brand recognition, it's like having an acquaintance—someone you know by name, but won't go much out of your way to engage. However, if the brand can be elevated to the level of becoming a "friend" . . . ? Well, you'll overlook your friends' imperfections. They may irritate you at times, but you'll still welcome them. They may even disappoint you, but you'll forgive them.

Apple would probably never have survived the recent transition from John Sculley to Gil Amelio to Steve Jobs without the friendship and affection it developed in the hearts of users over the years. The powerful bond that the brand created gave Apple the breathing room to develop a slew of new products, including the imaginative iMac, which was introduced in the fall of 1998 with astonishing early success. That, my friends, is the power of the brand. That's why the role of the brand shepherd is important, so important.

Myth 6: The Brand Is a Marketing Concept

All of our conversations about brands have to do with consumer perceptions and attitudes, advertising and marketing activities, competitive positioning, and all kinds of other marketing-related concepts. The people who care about brands are the brand or marketing managers, the advertising department, and the agency. People who talk about building or extending brands are writers and art directors, package and identity designers, researchers, and account planners. Therefore, the logical conclusion is that the brand is a marketing concept!

I'd like to challenge your thinking. There's another way to look at a brand. It's been increasingly recognized that brands have immense *financial* significance, and it can be argued that the whole

The brand is a marketing concept.

The Myth # 6

The brand is a financial concept.

The New Reality

concept of the value of a strong brand is primarily a financial one. Consider these facts:

- Brand equity (defined as the value of a corporation with its flagship brand names minus its value without them) is more and more viewed as a balance sheet item. In fact, in Britain, accounting principles allow brand equity to be classified as an asset on the balance sheet. As Alfred King, executive director of the NAA (the British equivalent of the U.S. FASB), wrote in *Management Accounting* in November 1990: "Brand names are more suited to balance sheet recognition as separate assets rather than as goodwill."
- Financial experts have calculated that the Marlboro cigarette brand alone represents about 40 percent of the entire valuation of the Philip Morris Company. That's some $40 billion of market capitalization attributable to the Marlboro brand itself!
- When Grand Metropolitan PLC acquired Pillsbury a few years back, it paid over six times book value. Sure, Grand Met was buying property, plant, and equipment, along with cash flow,

revenues, and profits. However, it seems clear that a huge contributor to the acquisition multiple Pillsbury brought was the proven power of brands like Pillsbury with its Pillsbury Doughboy, Green Giant, and Häagen-Dazs.

Here's a question: If you were to cut the Coca-Cola Company into two parts—one part that had all the plants and equipment, all the bottles, all the trucks, and all the other physical assets; and the other part with just the brand name, the logo, and the secret formula—which one would *you* want to own?

Let's look at some more recent examples. Take Amazon.com. In the first six months of 1998, the company's revenues were $204 million and they lost more than $30 million. But the market valuation of Amazon.com was about $5 billion! True, some of the valuation comes from the glamour of the Web, and some comes from investor euphoria, which will wear off in the morning; however, a good part of that valuation comes from the brand. 3Com paid $8.5 billion for US Robotics, a company with revenues of about $2 billion. Yes, it was buying access to broader distribution channels, more consumer-friendly products, and a stronger overall networking offering, but a significant part of the purchase price was for the PalmPilot brand, which subsequently became the Palm computer after a trademark dispute.

Every major example I have cited—Dell Computer, Intel, Microsoft, Sony, Hewlett-Packard, IBM—has created substantial financial value for stockholders by paying attention to its spectrum of brands. If the brand is more a financial asset than a vague marketing concept, shouldn't it deserve a little more respect? If it can add that much shareholder value, shouldn't the CEO have brand issues on his or her executive staff agenda?

With each of these myths I've addressed, I hope that you can see the power of the brand and that you are beginning to think about how you can apply the thinking in your own work.

4

The Marketing
Environment of
Technology—New Ways
of Working

Do You See Yourself?

Have your product life cycles shortened over the last 10 years? Are you beginning to see changes in distribution in your industry? Are there more mergers? Are there new kinds of alliances being formed? Are prices and costs falling for your product or service? Have you installed networked computer systems, relational databases, or virtual private networks (VPNs) in your company? Do your employees have easy access to the Internet? If you answered yes to any two of these questions, you will need to rethink your brand strategy.

What, you may ask, does a virtual private network (VPN) or a shorter–life cycle product have to do with your brand? "Branding is what my advertising department does with the agency," you say. "It has nothing to do with the core of my business." With all due respect, you are probably 100 percent wrong.

Impact of technology on brands—a checklist.

	Yes	No
1. Have your product life cycles shortened over the past 10 years?		
2. Are the distribution patterns beginning to change in your industry?		
3. Has there been an increase in merger activity in the past five years?		
4. Are new kinds of alliances and partnerships being formed in your industry?		
5. Are prices and costs falling for your products and services?		
6. Does your company have networked computer systems and relational databases?		
7. Does your company have, or is there an initiative to install, a virtual private network (VPN) or extranet?		
8. Do your employees have easy access to the Internet at your company?		
Score		

If you answered yes to any two questions,
you may need to reconsider your brand strategy.

The questions that I just asked have everything to do with brand. The clues as to what to do with the answers to these questions lie in the technology experience base of your company. Many of the successful technology brand builders have fought, and if not conquered, at least subdued what I call the pesky three key impediments to modern brand building: time compression, constant paradigm shifts, and decentralized organizational structures. More about these three demons later.

Let's go back to the introduction of the Sony PC. It took only nine months from the intent to the launch of a complicated product into a dynamic market. Contrast this with Gillette's launch of the Sensor razor. It took Gillette more than a year just to complete the research and development, which itself was based on years of direct consumer testing. It took another six months or more to develop a marketing plan, and many more months to launch a $50 million advertising blitz to establish the brand in the mind of the consumer.

When Bill Green, one of our senior strategists, worked for Procter & Gamble, a three- to five-year timetable for new product development and launch was not unusual. First, the company conducted extensive research to validate market potential. This was followed by a year or more of product development, testing, and refinement, including substantial consumer testing of various product alternatives. With a final consumer-validated product in hand, marketing development at last could begin its work—product naming, packaging, pricing analysis, marketing and advertising plans, and the selection of an advertising agency. No step was started before the previous one was completed. The entire process not only consumed tens of millions of dollars, but years of lead time.

This prototypical P&G approach generally worked—so you can't call it wrong for the time. However, even in the 1960s and 1970s, it was not unusual for competitors to steal P&G's thunder by moving more quickly and more aggressively to launch, sometimes reading P&G's own test market results as justification for a competitive launch of their own product.

The New Facts of Life

What are the new facts of marketing life? We have learned a lot observing our many technology clients over the years. The Sony PC introduction and the RenoAir turnaround, in which we participated, became catalysts for our understanding a kind of work life metabolism we had been unconsciously developing for years. During the course of this work, we uncovered those three pesky impediments to branding—time compression, constant change, and decentralized organizations—and what to do about them.

Time Compression

We've talked enough about time compression. It is simply a condition of doing business in the twenty-first century, and there is no option but to adjust. Something less than nine months from product concept (not advertising concept) to launch is not unusual. The PC industry is known for rapid obsolescence, much to the irritation of many consumers. Product life cycles are very short for PCs, some averaging only six months. Now, clients increasingly talk about web time, which means immediately. Without resorting to warp-speed branding, we'd be obsolete before we even launched.

Impediments to branding and what to do about them.

WHAT THE BRAND WANTS:	RELATIONSHIP OVER TIME	STABILITY	CONTROL
THE NEW REALITY:	TIME COMPRESSION	CONSTANT CHANGE	DECENTRALIZED ORGANIZATIONS
REMEDIES FOR IMPEDIMENTS:			
Concurrent work	✓	✓	
Communications flow	✓	✓	✓
Collaboration skills			
Recalibration process	✓	✓	✓
Flexibility	✓	✓	✓
Real-time decision making	✓	✓	
Comfort with ambiguity		✓	✓
Fluid and iterative process	✓	✓	
Respect for intuition	✓	✓	

Whatever is happening in high tech is only a precursor to what will happen to the rest of American industry, as product cycles become compressed and new technology keeps speeding up processes in the marketplace. If someone introduces a mountain bike, Schwinn can't wait 5 to 10 years—as it did previously—to alter its product line.

When sport-utility vehicles began catching on in the early 1990s, sparked by the innovative designs of the Nissan Pathfinder, the Jeep Cherokee, the Land Rover Discovery, and others, the big luxury cars held back. Then, in 1997, Mercedes and Lexus jumped into the fray. By mid-1998, the $35,000 Mercedes SUV and the $20,000-range Honda CR-V and Toyota RAV-4 sub-SUVs were eating up market share in America; still, General Motors had not developed competing models for its Cadillac, Buick, Oldsmobile, Pontiac, or Saturn lines.

The issue is not just speed in manufacturing. It's also a question of how long it takes to amass the massive capital and intellectual resources necessary to come out with a new line. However you describe the issue, it comes down to being able to move light-years faster than we did 20 years ago when most of the captains of American industry were earning their spurs in middle management.

Decentralized Organizations to Move Fast

Getting a product or service to market quickly—increasingly an absolute requirement for success—is requiring more and more of every group involved in the process. The demand for speed simply won't allow anything else. The traditional system of sequential decision making is disappearing and is being replaced by a much more organic process of concurrent development, cycling, and recycling in real time.

Concurrent development typically means decentralized teams, often in different locations, different time zones, even different countries, as I illustrated by our Sony experience. These teams are working on different aspects of the project simultaneously, and

Decentralized organization structure—a typical technology company.

◀ Software development teams
■ Manufacturing locations
◗ Strategic partners
● Corporate headquarters
◆ Division headquarters

one group's activities will have a major influence on others. Has engineering discovered that marketing's need for a certain feature can't be accommodated in the time frame? Has a significant competitive development changed the landscape into which the product will launch, with resulting needs for engineering changes? Is there an unexpected shortage of a key component that will reduce available product quantities, or even delay the launch?

Communication and Recalibration–Essential to Teams

In this environment, it's important to be sure that all the interdependencies of the project are understood from the beginning, and that constant recalibration is an integral part of the team process. Members of the team from every discipline need to participate in all major planning sessions to be certain every perspective is heard.

Advertising seems to be a catalyst for this kind of broad review. Maybe it's because everyone has an opinion about advertising or because advertising cuts across every part of a project that it takes on this role. Maybe it's because we have already been sensitized to these issues, and as a result, we influence this to happen almost unconsciously.

Whatever the reason, it's not surprising for our agency to walk into an advertising presentation in a decentralized client organization and find just about *everyone* there: engineering, product marketing, strategic marketing, customer marketing, sales, customer support, human resources, investor relations, general management, and, yes, the communications professionals, too! This hodgepodge of a decision-making body, fueled by everyone's interest in what our advertising's going to be, is actually an important part of the recalibration mechanism. Advertising may be the official subject of the meeting, but our experience has been that this group interaction often bubbles up critical pieces of information that go far beyond advertising alone—information that is vital to the entire project and hasn't yet been widely shared.

Recently, we were in a large meeting with a satellite-based global telecommunications service company. The meeting included the client's marketing, communications, and operations people; its equity and service provider partners from around the world; and four different communications agencies. The meeting's purpose was to focus on the definition of the client's brand around the world. It was at that meeting that we all discovered a significant piece of new information. The start of the company's service had been delayed by several months because of a glitch in the satellite launch schedule in Kazakhstan, and most of the people in the room did not know it.

For another telecommunications client, after weeks of intense work, we were presenting creative concepts for what had been declared Priority 1—a new product that was scheduled to be launched in the next quarter. We were discussing the merits of one creative approach against another when the company president— who reviews all advertising plans—asked a stunning question: "Why are you worrying about *that* product? All your efforts and all our spending has to be behind this other product that'll be ready next month!" No one else in the room appeared to know anything about this mysterious new product, much less its priority. More than anything, this failure to communicate, so critical to this decentralized way of working, provided real obstacles to a successful launch. In the end, there wasn't enough time to ready a sensible campaign for the new product, and the company put the launch of the original product on hold.

We've had many such situations over time when, in advertising meetings involving cross-functional teams, we all find out together about a manufacturing delay in Japan; or a new study of costs of ownership that will change our message completely; or, as once happened with Hewlett-Packard, an unexpected engineering breakthrough that would completely change the value proposition of a new product.

With decentralization comes a deconstruction of tasks. For example, watch any weekend sporting event on television and you'll see several pieces of information flashing on the screen at once. Part of the screen is given to scores, another part to game statistics—and sometimes they even leave a little room for the game. All the information is pushed to the viewer simultaneously. It would be a great disservice if advertising and marketing professionals ignored this within their own operations. To some—often clients—the barrage of data is maddening. To others—mostly young, computer-savvy customers—this kind of multimessaging is a familiar, everyday life form.

Simultaneous messages and decentralized functions shape and instruct our ability to manage assignments, to access information, and to understand the tangible attributes of the products and services we're being asked to brand. As decentralization increases, demand for brand strategies comes under more pressure, because of the many different things happening all at once. Like a universe that is spinning and expanding at the same time, it becomes essential to maintain a clear and cohesive brand strategy in such a chaotic environment. As corporate demands on the brand multiply, all phases of brand building must be done in concert. Try implementing that without a clear idea of what the brand strategy is—you'll end up with 20 of them, and none will be correct.

In a sense, to be successful today you have to embody a contradiction. On the one hand, you must accept that decentralized authority is a barrier to orderly branding, but on the other, you must recognize that decentralization makes it imperative that you possess a clear and consistent idea of what the brand is and what it stands for. Your job as supervisor is to lead while knowing that you have no definite mandate. Technology has upset all the rules of respect and order. Live with it. Linear movements, like promotions, aren't enough to keep great talent coming back for more work. You're going to need the passion and zeal of an evangelist to attract smart people capable of overcoming the obstacles to building great brands.

Working with technology companies has pushed the concept of the project to the forefront of the creative process. This is a result of necessity in the tech world, in which individuals perform a variety of functions because of limited budgets and limited time. Projects are shepherded by those who believe in them, not by those who are simply assigned to them. Titles mean less and less, results count for more. Passion and excitement drive the team of people, not a top-down sense of orders and rules. Most new hires are too busy to be even bothered about rules. They have been raised to solve problems by getting connected on their own, rather than figuring out whom to ask first.

The advent of e-mail, electronic bulletin boards, and Internet-based information has fostered a sense of community that does not respect geographic—or corporate—boundaries. Seeking out experts in a particular field is no longer a process of going up the chain of command to get to the right person. It is being able to reach hundreds of possible experts all over the world through a single e-mail. Technology not only has given us the means to do this, but encouraged us to be comfortable with such a process. The transfer of data becomes a collegial, decentralized event, and marketing and advertising professionals are going to have to learn to work in this kind of environment.

Redesign Work Processes to Do Things Concurrently

The speed of technologic change forces marketing and advertising professionals to swap linear, hierarchical methods of building brands for rapid-fire, team-oriented approaches. Because technology breeds short product cycles, it makes us develop advertising and marketing right along with the products and services being offered. This is the basis for concurrent work. To the inexperienced it might also seem random. Brand building—along with the accompanying marketing and advertising strategies—is no longer an afterthought or an end result; rather, it is put together like the pieces of a puzzle—borrowing, adding, and subtracting as products and services get closer and closer to market.

Unlike a traditional consumer packaged-goods company, because of the compressed time frame in a technology company, information from the consumer informs both the advertising and the product design just about simultaneously. We are often developing brand strategies and designing ads at the same time as the engineers are still designing some of the features of the product. As a result, the marketing rocket is lit much earlier in the process. No longer do communications professionals (including public relations, collateral producers, channel marketers, web specialists, as well as advertising people) step in at the end of a product's design, gather round a conference table, and figure out what to do with the latest box of wires, chips, and buttons.

By cutting the time—and the cost—needed to get a product into the marketplace, rapid prototyping forces the branding machinery to kick into gear much sooner. At Chrysler's rapid-prototype lab in Detroit, machines running around the clock spit out all kinds of automotive objects, such as dashboards and transmissions, which can turn three months of bending steel into a week of molding plastic. Using rapid-prototype machines helped reduce the design and manufacturing interval by six months.

The speed of technological change means information from the marketplace has to be assimilated much earlier into the brand strategy, and adds to the complexity. Products now have to become more responsive and personal to customers, and so do the people charged with brand building. Tennis rackets with a grip personalized to fit an individual's hand or Christmas ornaments designed on request on a computer—all are the result of a technology application.

Flatten the Organization to Work Collaboratively

Check out how technology companies operate. They can teach marketing and advertising executives a bit about the very way business is conducted. Elaborate planning meetings and deeply rooted corporate hierarchies are of little use if they don't foster critical thinking and discussion about the marketplace and the brand. The innovative ideas that drive technology brands don't come from one place inside the company. They are the result of a collaborative approach, which embodies chaos as much as traditional brand building tries to embody predictability.

Even the physical space of workers has to change to enable faster collaboration. Few technology companies of any standing have the time to indulge in the traditional perks of corporate gluttony. Manifestations of size (the big office, the traditional corridors of power, parking spaces, executive bathrooms, executive dining rooms) are replaced by work groups and information centers that encourage fertile productivity. At Hewlett-Packard, CEO Lew Platt admittedly has a nice-sized office with a picture window that overlooks an internal garden. His office, however, has no door, and the office itself is part of a larger complex of executive offices with a large central waiting area. You do not get the feeling that you are standing so much in a corner of power, as at the center of a large enterprise that has many moving parts, all trying to stay in sync. There is an unassuming quality about the physical scale of the place—a certain egalitarian atmosphere, which I find commonplace in Silicon Valley. At many California companies, the CEO doesn't even have an office. Instead, he or she occupies an open cubicle, similar to those of the people around.

The paramount struggle for anyone supervising the new roller-blading, tattooed, and multicolor-haired knowledge workers is how to integrate them into existing office cultures. Quite literally, you are going to have to shake up the office furniture. You can't have conversations that offer everyone an equal amount of floor time, sitting in the boss's office, or staring at the same old walls. New kinds of workers require upsetting the hierarchy of the traditional world.

You will never get to new ways of defining brands without new management communications and new, higher levels of interconnectivity. Chances are these will all come via technology. As much as technology is feared or misunderstood by people born before Pac-Man, it is a way of life for those who are constantly being asked to program their parents' VCR.

Collaboration Requires Different Workforce Skills

If multiple groups are working concurrently on different, but related, parts of a project, with the objective of getting it to market faster, there is nothing more important than the effective collaboration of team members. Sounds easy, right? At first glance, you might think it's just a matter of scheduling periodic review meetings and providing some technology tools to facilitate real-time information sharing.

These are important, of course. However, there's an even more critical element in the move toward collaborative, high-speed work styles—that's the new skill sets required of team leaders. Great managers and great *individual* contributors are not always the most effective people to lead a highly collaborative environment, because they may not have some of the special skills needed to drive others and the project to success. What personal skill sets are vital in high-speed, collaborative activities?

- *Great interpersonal communication skills:* We're not talking about presentation skills or being a good writer or speaker; rather, we mean having the ability to listen, understand, clarify, and communicate clearly with others (often in a charged environment). There's a premium on being able to synthesize and summarize multiple points of view, to seek and reach agreement within the group, and, especially, to gauge the magnitude and structure of communications required to keep everyone up to speed, clear about objectives, timing, and next steps. If you're not hearing a lot of this kind of talk from your leader—"Did you remember to tell Jack about that change?" "Let's give Kim a heads-up on that one, because it might impact her packaging development schedule." "Have the folks in New Jersey agreed to that faster timetable?"—something's wrong.

- *Flexibility:* The team is moving very fast, concurrently developing strategies and plans that used to be sequentially organized, and making real-time decisions as they go. There is an abundance of data, but essential information may be coming late to the process—or possibly not at all. Developments in one area will impact others, and they can even dictate changes in plans that have already been put to bed. In this fast-paced environment, rigid, inflexible attitudes and behaviors simply don't work. Team members need to recognize that ownership of the project, and even its component parts, is really the team's, not the individual's, prerogative. There is so much interdependency, with information and priorities changing in a tight time frame, that skill sets must be integrated and flexibility is essential.

- *Real-time decision making:* Team members must be able to think and work on the fly, synthesizing incomplete information to create the best available solution, and they must be able to quickly see the impact of new developments on their areas and on the overall project. Highly analytical, "check, check again, and then recheck" processes take too long and won't work, because some of the facts are likely to change while the decision is being checked! There's a real premium on identifying team members who are comfortable with real-time decision making.

■ *Comfort with near-permanent ambiguity:* Information flow is always uneven, and especially so when it is being delivered in real time, so different people have slightly different sets of information at any point in time. Important information may not even be available when at least a preliminary decision must be made. Team members need to be able to recognize this ambiguity, not find it frustrating to the point of paralysis, and be able to function effectively with less-than-complete data. Some people thrive in this environment, whereas others find it chaotic and paralyzing.

As we talk with different groups within a client, receiving sometimes widely divergent perspectives about objectives, market situations, priorities, the competition, and other critical issues, we have learned that ambiguity is a given. Some of this is a permanent part of the landscape, but Winkler tries to play a leading role in minimizing the impact—helping teams sift through contradictory data or points of view to reach consensus and necessary focus.

When our agency began working with CyberStar, Loral's new satellite-based data communications company, we interviewed the senior management group and found widely divergent views of the company's fundamental business goals. Not surprisingly, because satellite communications were just becoming commercialized, the company was brand new, and not everyone was pointed in the same direction. We shared this input across the management team, helping to define the fundamentals of what service Cyber-Star was offering and what its positioning should be.

Similarly, in introducing the Sony Notebook PC, it was immediately clear that there were dual objectives—introduction of the product itself *and* the need to begin positioning Sony and its VAIO platform as the leader in the coming convergence of computers, communications, and entertainment. Each of the products that would operate under this VAIO umbrella—PCs, displays, printers, digital cameras, and more—had a separate product-marketing team, separate budgets, and separate business objectives. They didn't work together much, they didn't share much information, and how these individual products would fit together under the VAIO platform was pretty fuzzy.

Still, Sony's long-term strategy made it important that this ambiguity be reduced; therefore, we got the East and West Coast product-marketing groups for each product together in a room for the first time. Winkler executives led a series of problem-solving exercises, which led to the development of a brand promise: "Only Sony helps you marry information, entertainment, and communications to explore your passions." At the end of this daylong meeting, we felt we had made tremendous strides in gaining a common insight and understanding of what Sony needed to do and what we needed to help them with.

We also developed a comprehensive message architecture that showed how application, product, and brand messages could work together under the overall brand promise. For the first time, we were able to get agreement from all product-marketing managers to pool their individual advertising budgets to support platform-based, as opposed to product-based, advertising. This advertising combined the VAIO capabilities with specific products to present a picture of the freedom and creativity that Sony helps to support—"Because You Can." A secondary benefit of this way of working was that the client was very bought into the strategy. The actual campaign development went very quickly and very smoothly with almost no last-minute changes.

For the movie *Godzilla*, no images of Godzilla himself were available until the actual release of the film! Imagine trying to create advertising, promotional tie-ins, and merchandising materials to promote the movie without being able to see or show the gigantic hero. It's very analogous to putting together advertising plans for a product that neither you nor anyone else has ever seen, and you are working only with a verbal concept. Now, there's working with ambiguity.

How to Deal with Ambiguity–A Fact of Warp-Speed Life

Increasingly, this situation of not knowing exactly what's going on, but having to deal with it anyway, will be the rule rather than the exception. We teach our people to expect the frustration of incomplete information, and to recognize that their work may not be perfect from the start but will be fixed as we go along. This causes us to focus even more on concepts at the brand level, because the details will be shifting throughout the process. Some of the ways we do this in the agency are through tissue sessions and heavy information flow.

Tissue Sessions to Calibrate Early

Team members must feel comfortable sharing preliminary, half-baked ideas with colleagues very early in the process. Opening up this kind of dialog is vital to encourage new input, draw out new information, and establish a continuing process of recalibration as the project moves forward. At Winkler, we place great emphasis on what we call *tissue sessions* with clients, inviting them to join our creative and planning teams in thinking about preliminary strategies and emerging creative concepts. Ideas are shown in very rough form, as quickly sketched black-and-white tissues, not as finished materials. This helps us all focus on the relevance, power, and extendability of a concept, not on the artwork itself. It makes it easier for all of us to talk about how an idea might impact the target we're after, and not whether the color of the visual should be blue instead of green. For this process to work best, people in the meeting—especially those who actually developed the rough idea to expose to the group—have to learn to be comfortable sharing their initial thinking without major defensiveness. They have to appreciate that a good early idea may get even better with new input and perspectives, and that one element of Concept A might combine with another part of Concept B to make an even more powerful Concept C! Our best clients understand that they are being invited early into a fragile creative process, so they are respectful and tactful in the discussions.

Information Flow Is Critical

Rapid market or product changes, new account planning input, new timetables—all the ambiguity of a concurrent, high-speed

Tissue sessions.

process makes it essential that information that is as up-to-date as possible flow rapidly within the team all the time. Technology is a major factor in achieving this requirement, of course. At Winkler, we use e-mail and voice mail, centralized files with a database behind them for easier searching, 100 percent Internet access on every desktop, password-protected client home pages on the World Wide Web, a videoconferencing facility at the agency, and more. We have even built a proprietary Web-based software tool called TeamToolz™, which facilitates collaboration, communications, and project management between Winkler, the client, and other specialized agencies that are part of the marketing communications team supporting the client's brand (more about this in Chapter 6).

Beyond technology, plain, old, face-to-face human contact—getting individuals and teams physically together—leads to an organic process of information flow and sharing, with intense discussions leading to real agreements. E-mail is great for disseminating information quickly, but it's not a tool for interaction or discussion. In fact, we have a rule at the agency—no more than two e-mail messages on any one subject. After two e-mails, if there's still confusion, get together and hash it out face-to-face!

Intuitive versus Rational Decision Making

Technology companies have taught us that we can trust intuition, and gigantic bets are made on intuition. The Venture Capitalists (VCs), located in VC Gulch, on Sand Hill Road in Menlo Park, California, have created trillions of dollars of corporate value based mainly on intuition. No matter what's in a business plan for a brand new idea for a whole new industry—you can't prove it! Today, even the VCs look at business plans differently. They should be short and to the point. Plans no longer need to be four inches thick, because detailed predictions of the future are a total waste of time. Show them the concept, the environment, and the talent—they'll figure out their bets—largely based on intuition.

The VC leaders don't have the luxury of basing their decisions on logic or market tests. What's there to test when an idea is so new that people have a tough time even absorbing it? Instead, decisions are based on a presumption of need. Big money is funding this intuition, and for the veterans who survive, the good bets more than make up for the failures.

Ten years ago, you would have had to wheel in facts and figures—tons of them—at a senior-level meeting. Today, it is acceptable to say "My gut says. . . . ," or "My sense of it is. . . ." That's a radically different way of operating—and huge decisions are made this way. Even Intel's Andy Grove admits that the company's shift away from memory chips to chips that provided speed and processing power was a gamble. The company staked its future on going left instead of right, and Grove has said in interviews that the decision, while informed, was not preordained for success.

Fluid and Iterative versus Process Oriented

Here again, this nonlinear approach owes much to the random nature of how information can be gleaned from the computer. Being able to quickly click around, to search for information based on need, rather than to follow page numbers, offers more choices and unpredictable results. The linking and browsing aspects of the video game generation are embedded in the thinking patterns of the new consumer and the new employee. It would be disastrous to try to change this; rather, it is vital that marketing and advertising leaders harness the new processes and bend them to the interest of their clients.

Although most consumer product companies would never permit a product unfinished by consumer standards to leave their factory, a technology company presents a new set of demands. Not only will it constantly revise and update its products, it will seek customer feedback to determine exactly what the next version of the product should be. In some circles it becomes a ubiquitous beta version—a test version that never becomes final. For technology companies, this means routine distribution of unfinished products, with follow-on attention given to incorporating updates and changes based on customer demand. The sophisticated consumer will demand changes, even fundamental changes, and the company will respond in a hurry.

In the traditional, process-oriented world, change is the enemy of the corporate structure. That is why traditional branding strategies have little ability to cope with change. But the technology world, driven by innovation, teaches us to embrace change. It forces us to respond to chaos and tension, the natural by-products of change. Decisions are made and remade in a fluid, networked way—just like computer networks, in which every computer can talk to any other computer without regard to hierarchy or central control.

As speed increases to take in variables, such as different kinds of technology, shifting markets, changing customer bases, and even new industry structures, there is the need for greater flexibility in the branding system. What is true today about your customer may be radically different two quarters from now. The branding system must recognize that change and be able to respond. It is easy to be fooled into thinking that constant movement in the market requires tinkering with a brand. Each iteration of the brand must be sensitive to the connections already in place. We'll talk more about this in Chapter 7 ("The Brand Ecosystem").

The Power of Emotion

What are you doing inside your organization to create the emotional energy necessary for innovation? Are you closing the distance between ideas and action? Is it possible to turn the chaos of new people and new ways of communicating into a passion linked to the organization's goals?

Technology enterprises have infused branding with energy that borders on the fanatical. Their products are sometimes prosaic, but their passionate attachment to "changing the world" reveals a methodology based on emotional belief rather than traditional market-testing techniques. Apple has coined a job title now found in many Silicon Valley companies—the "Evangelist." This crusading attitude has even penetrated the consumer market. A 1996 survey of 1,000 households with personal computers performed by Lexmark International for Roger Starch Worldwide, showed that a majority of Americans would rather give up something else than part with their computers.

Insane? Perhaps, but it's time brand builders begin to mirror the committed consumer's excitement.

5

Advertising Agencies– Dinosaurs or New Genetic Creatures?

A s work styles are changing from industry to industry, advertising agencies, still prime movers in the branding world, need to begin to rethink their own work processes. Take our agency's creative development process. Some time ago, we used the classic linear advertising process in which work gets handed off from department to department.

In this style of working, account service wrote a creative strategy based on the client's input and some existing research data. Usually this research was "archaeological," as some of our planners like to refer to it. This means it is an analysis of how the consumer behaved in the past. We convened focus groups to uncover how the consumer felt about the product. An insensitive moderator, however, or the occasional disrupting effect of group dynamics could easily skew results. The answers these groups gave us rarely uncovered deep insights that would allow us to accurately predict future customer behavior.

When the creative strategy was written and approved by the client, it got handed off to the creative department, which then had to produce creative work on deadline, usually without any first-hand experience of the consumer, without much time to ruminate on what was in the strategy or to challenge it. Small wonder there is so much bad advertising.

After much angst, the creative department would develop a campaign of finished storyboards and layouts. In the meantime, the media department was asked, "Where should this stuff run?" It would then work up a media plan to meet the objectives and budget. Lo and behold, it's time to get ready for the client presentation and we find that the media department is proposing 60-second radio spots and single pages in lifestyle magazines, whereas the creative department has been developing a TV campaign with magazine spreads and billboards. There's a mad, last-minute scramble to reorganize the presentation. Everyone's unhappy, veiled threats are exchanged that this better never happen again—and off everyone runs to the client to put on a good show of agency solidarity and support for the work. The client has to buy it because we're on deadline.

The client, in the meantime, was sitting around wondering what is happening. "We briefed these guys three months ago. What the hell is going on? I'm getting nervous. My boss is asking me if we are ready for the launch. It would be nice to have the advertising, collateral, and point of purchase coordinated creatively. No time though. We're late—we'll need to use the boutique down the street. Maybe they'll come up with a tag line we can use for the sales meeting. Maybe we can use it in the ads—it'll be out there already. What am I going to do if the campaigns they bring aren't right?"

Sound familiar? These common and unhappy results on both the client and the agency side are often the by-products of what is a totally outmoded process for developing smart advertising.

It had its place for decades, when our world was more orderly. When the mass market was just that—a reasonably homogeneous market in which the consumer had reasonably predictable life patterns; when product choice was measured over a handful of brands, rather than hundreds or even thousands; and when information about new products was limited to a standard spectrum of media (i.e., local newspapers and radio, magazines, and three television networks). In retrospect, life seemed simpler then. Today, many veterans of the ad agency world say to me, "The business isn't fun anymore." I disagree. The part that's not fun is working with a process that just doesn't match today's business reality.

How We Changed Our Process: What We've Learned from Our Clients

Let me contrast the old way of working with how Winkler Advertising works with its clients today. Who gets to market fastest wins! Speed provides the spoils, and the pace satisfies the adrenaline junkies.

Today, at Winkler, the development of a creative strategy is a multidisciplinary team approach, with account service, creative, media, and account planning all playing central roles from the very beginning of the process. Often the teams regroup on strategies and plans as market situations and client needs change during the process! As strategy is so important, let's take a moment to discuss the role of account planning.

Account Planning to Create a Knowledge Framework

Strategy has to start with client input, of course, but account planning is increasingly important to our accounts, and it plays a unique role in crafting more effective strategies and executions. Account planning represents the voice of the customers, not the agency or the client; the process of looking into their minds to gain insight into attitudes, beliefs, and feelings that influence brand selection is vital to the crafting of smart advertising. Our planners have sat with PC users and video game players in their homes for Sony and Eidos Interactive. They've talked with passengers in airport lounges and flown with them on RenoAir. As a result, they bring a real understanding of what's going on in the consumer's mind, and gut, to help shape strategies and creative work that taps that nerve of emotion and leads to successful work.

Planners are proactive partners with account management and creatives. There is, in effect, an interdependent, interdisciplinary approach to strategic development in which planners play a key role. Planners provide consumer and brand insight, help craft the strategy, and work closely with creative people to ensure that executions capture the strategy and communicate it persuasively. Our creative brief, for example, is the responsibility of the planners, but it is, in fact, crafted with heavy input from both creative, media, and account service. All disciplines must sign off on the final strategy.

How is account planning different from market research? Here's a way to describe this relatively new form of advertising research, which fits especially well with warp-speed branding.

We have found that account planning helps us move faster, because we already have a framework of understanding to work with.

Research versus account planning.

	RESEARCH	VERSUS	ACCOUNT PLANNING
Involvement:	Ad hoc/passive		Continuous/active
Direction:	An end in itself		An aid to judgments
Orientation:	Measurement/technique		Applications of the results
Passion for:	Facts and certainties		Hypotheses and possibilities
Bottom line:	Information		Meaning
Focus:	What has been done		What can be done

RenoAir: How We Applied Warp-Speed Work Style
RenoAir, our client, competes on the West Coast with Southwest, Shuttle by United, and Alaska Airlines. The airline had struggled, losing $24 million in its 1997 fiscal year, and was experiencing declining revenue and load factors over the first two quarters of 1998. Several reasons accounted for this decline:

- Brutal competition on the West Coast—in nearly every market that RenoAir competes, there was a better-known competitor with a better schedule.
- Ticket prices overall were very low in this cutthroat market.
- On-time performance and maintenance problems lead to heavy flight cancellations for Reno.
- Not enough reservation agents to answer the phones resulted in 30 percent of callers hanging up.
- Lower advertising budgets than competitors.
- A perception that the airline provided poor customer service and has poor internal morale.

Faced with these operational and perceptual problems, an entirely new management team was brought in by the board of directors in early 1998, led by Joe O'Gorman, a seasoned airline executive. Winkler Advertising joined the team a few months later.

The agency's creative, account management, media, and account planning teams, working as a group, set out to confirm current customer attitudes and uncover the real motivations for driving purchasing decisions in the West Coast short-haul airline market.

We found out some interesting things that most frequent travelers already know, but somehow have not penetrated the consciousness of most airlines. First off, air travel is viewed as a "necessary evil" by most travelers. Most airlines (with the exception of Alaska Airlines) fare poorly in terms of customer service. Fliers feel there is a lack of respect for them as paying customers, especially relative to other service industries. In addition, traveling consumers are very savvy to the fact that what airlines say (advertise) and what they do are not in sync. Advertising messages, therefore, are ignored and are considered unbelievable overall.

Faced with this situation, the group's conclusion—led by the insights of account planners who flew RenoAir routes and talked to customers and employees—was that RenoAir's product is really its employees. No amount of advertising to the flying public will ever change the fact that consumers are too often forced to interact with nonmotivated/uncaring employees. Our solution? Focus our communication efforts not on the people ultimately purchasing tickets . . . but on the employees of RenoAir!

Our rationale was simple: If we could change their mindset and make them believe the company really cares about them, employee enthusiasm would improve. Better yet, if these messages were placed in media seen by consumers, it would send an "indirect" and, therefore, more credible message that the company was working to improve service and morale. The flying public would be getting a peek into the inner workings of a company in transition. Who doesn't like an underdog?

The creative work began, initially at the branding level. Midway through the creative development process, however, it became clear that RenoAir, in its quest to put "butts in seats," needed advertising that worked on two levels immediately:

1. "Brand" advertising that began to change RenoAir's image and made people feel better about them as an airline option (as outlined previously).
2. Tactical ads focused on specific promotions, fare sales, new routes, and so on, in more traditional media vehicles.

What started out as a brand assignment resulted in a reality that required 21 ads concepted in two weeks, produced in four days,

RenoAir campaign.

Introducing
the 500 mph
chairlift.

Looking for a quick ride to the slopes? Well, you've found it. We have the best on-time record in the

business. And offer perks like American Airlines AAdvantage Miles and first-class upgrades for as little

as $30. Which just about guarantees that the only thing more impressive than the trip up to the mountain

is going to be the trip down. Visit us at www.renoair.com. Or call your travel agent or 1-800-RENO AIR.

RenoAir
Change is in the air

RenoAir campaign.

From Silicon Valley
to Silicone Valley
four times a day.

Whether you're into screenplays or software, you'll love our new non-stops between San Jose and

Burbank. You'll get American Airlines AAdvantage Miles and $30 first-class upgrades. Just have your

people contact our people. Visit us at www.renoair.com. Or call your travel agent or 1-800-RENO AIR.

RenoAir
Change is in the air

RenoAir campaign.

If you can make it to
the airport on time,
why can't your flight?

Something's up at Reno Air. Find out what next week.

RenoAir

Assigned seating.
It's just one of those
things that separate air
travel from bus travel.

Something's up at Reno Air. Find out what next week.

RenoAir

Sure your call
is important to that
other airline. That's why
they put their best
machine on it.

Something's up at Reno Air. Find out what next week.

RenoAir

113

and rotated through 14 markets. The program was augmented with about 8 radio ads, all to be produced on the same schedule.

Once again, the planning, account management, media, and creative groups came together to strategize against these midstream course corrections. It was agreed that the best way to accomplish both objectives was to use our tactical advertising to positively impact the business right away, but to create advertising with a vision for a bigger brand effort down the road. We needed to begin to integrate advertising, which in the past could be considered "one offs" through a common look and feel of all the airline's communications. Even more important, we needed to provide a sense in the promotions that RenoAir was becoming a very different airline.

We all agreed there was no better way to communicate the change than through the use of intelligent humor. This attitude would deal with consumers' negative perceptions about us in a credible way, would make the most of limited funds, and would convey an air of confidence that we had lacked historically.

Early returns were very promising: our first "low, low fare" ad in this new style generated in two days 12,500 more reservation bookings than previous ads, or $450,000 in additional revenue!

Twenty-One Ads in Four Days?

The elements of working well in warp speed start with the team concept. The multidisciplinary team includes account service, planning, creative, media traffic, and production. Besides being able to think and act fast, teams afford the agency the ability to rotate people on a given client without disturbing the history and knowledge on the business that is shared by *all* the team members. Another important part of the work style is that the client can talk to anyone on the team—not just the account executive, who in a traditional agency acts as the gatekeeper.

Through experience and trial and error we have found that there are four things to watch to make teams work and we organized the RenoAir team this way.

1. Constant communication
2. Processes
3. Streamlining
4. Technology

Constant Communication

There are several elements of good communication that we found most useful. The first is our open-plan environment—no walled offices—to keep the informal flow of information going. E-mail becomes a useful way to quickly document client conversations and send them out to the whole team so that everyone is on the same page. When possible, teams sit together so that they can catch each other immediately.

Processes

We have trained our RenoAir client to make requests as much as possible by e-mail, so the entire team is informed simultaneously. The account executive prepares a daily "Hot List" by e-mail, so that retail ads going into multiple geographies with prices and schedule changes frequently can be tracked daily. Our weekly status meeting with the client can then focus on bigger issues such as how the business is doing. Are any markets in trouble? What has worked and what hasn't? And other issues.

Streamlining

Whenever we could, we streamlined processes. The campaign itself had a campaign brief to guide each execution, but individual ads got a tactical directive attached to the campaign brief. This way we had an overall strategy that didn't need to get reinvented with each ad. We also adopted a media rotation chart, rather than a traditional flowchart, so that we knew on a day-by-day basis which ad was to run where. This allowed us to make quick media schedule changes if a price had to change to respond to competitive pressure. Finally, we adopted electronic mechanical distribution to all newspapers and digital radio distribution to shave more time.

Technology

As you have already read, we use e-mail, videoconferencing, and TeamToolz, a sophisticated extranet for sharing and storing information in a collaborative work environment (see Chapter 6). We have also adopted many new production processes, using state-of-the-art technology to get work done more quickly and to be able to respond to last-minute changes.

1. Often, we have a rush photo or illustration that's required. We now have access to a lot of digital stock photography, which has already been scanned in high resolution, converted to CMYK for print, color-corrected, and retouched. Our art buyer will search the digital stock houses on-line first to save time and money. Depending on the size of the files, we can download them off the digital stock houses' web sites.

2. Most of the illustrators can e-mail their electronic illustrations to us, which saves time and money as well. Both are critical in rush, retail work.

3. If a photo shoot is required and no time is available to send casting or head shots to the client, we can convert the shots to electronic low-resolution JPEG files or PDFs (portable document format) and e-mail them to the client(s) to open and view the potential talent and make comments. We use the same process for viewing rough work in progress.

4. If this is a rush photo shoot situation with multiple people in the approval cycle on the client side, after the shoot, we can also place our recommended transparency on the Web for all

to immediately look at for content (not color). The old way, which would have taken at least three days, would have been to make duplicate transparencies and send one to each client at each location.

5. Once the mechanicals are completed in-house and the client has approved them, we can instantly upload our new or revised mechanicals to our vendors' FTP sites, their web servers from which they can instantly retrieve the files, pull them off, and begin production with no downtime. Bye-bye slow messengers!

6. If we need a low-resolution file of the retoucher's work, we can pull those files off their FTP site and give them to the studio to place for position only in the mechanical. We can also e-mail these low-resolution retouched or composited files to our clients if they need to see and approve something at the last minute and there isn't time (or money) to generate a color proof. Although the color viewed on the monitor/display is not accurate, it is often adequate for approval with more "trusting" clients.

7. To save three to four hours of film prep time, we have selected digital prepress shops that have digital proofing devices (such as the Kodak "Approval" proof), which accurately produce proofs depicting how the four-color image will look once ink hits paper. However, they can do this in one-quarter to one-half the time, because four pieces of film don't need to be generated to create the proof. This also saves money (about 50 percent), and we are able to see the revisions that much faster.

8. If we need to show a client a last-minute proof of a four-color image that was retouched, we are able to create a PDF file of the visual and text and e-mail it to the client for them to see. The color won't be *exactly* correct, but it will be close enough and good enough for general content.

9. In rush retail situations, once we have approved the com-posed- or stripped-color proof, our digital prepress shop cre-ates PDF files of the high-res files and sends all the files via T1s (usually Whamnet!) to all the publications or their print-ers for electronic pickup, plating, and printing.
10. If we have too much work for one shop to handle in the time frame, we will have them use high-speed T1 lines to send the files to a sister shop to produce and return via T1.

All of these tools to speed the back end help us make more time for front-end creative concept development.

New Behavior Surrounds Us

The story of one advertising agency's relocation processes, 10 years apart, is a graphic illustration of the changes in work style evident in many industries. In early 1988, we made our decision to move to San Francisco to be closer to the creative community and to the infrastructure of our own advertising industry. We approached the situation systematically and with great attention to preplanning. We were lucky enough to find our space in the South of Market area very quickly. It was a sublease from Bank of America, with a fabulous panoramic view of the Bay, quite a treat for us after the endless expanse of concrete buildings and parking lots of the Golden Triangle in Silicon Valley. Because we owned our own building in Silicon Valley, we had the luxury of time—we did not have a date by which we had to be out of our existing offices—just an internal clock. We hired our architect, who hired a space plan-ner. We saw several iterations of space layouts and made the appropriate compromises based on budget.

Then the architect hired the contractor and work began. We carefully planned all the logistics of the move and were set to go.

One small problem—the carpet mill failed to meet its deadline, and the carpet wouldn't be ready on time. The contractor's bid was coming in way over the budget, and we were behind on the construction. We had just landed a big new account and had to hire a few more people, so the space plan had to be revised. Back and forth it went in its slow, methodical pace. The move itself was a nightmare—the carpet came in after the furniture; the networking cable people came in behind the phone people and pulled out all the phone cables while they were doing their work; and on and on and on.

Flash Forward to 1996

Times are good: we are now four times bigger, the pace is faster, and we are very busy with many clients like Sony and Hewlett-Packard depending on us. Eidos Interactive has a slew of TV commercials it wants produced. There is no downtime. However, we have to get out of our space as we are bursting at the seams and our lease is up. The San Francisco office space market was the tightest it had been in a decade, so there was very little inventory to look at. We also wanted a space that would accommodate an open environment, so we spent a frustrating three months looking at building after building, floor after floor, with no success. Finally, in late October 1996, we found 25,000 square feet of space in an ideal location with a 360-degree view of the city, including the San Francisco Bay from Alcatraz to the South Bay, plus an outdoor deck—unheard of in high-rise buildings in San Francisco! There was only one tiny problem: We had to be out of our current offices by March 1, 1997, and the new space was an undeveloped shell! We had four short months to make it happen.

The architectural firm we selected, based on past work and a very quick "spec" concept for the space, was Jong & Jong in Berkeley. Their work fit our "cheap and edgy" brief. They had demonstrated creativity in their use of materials, texture, and color to create a rich-looking environment without pretension or exorbitant cost. (We prefer to spend money on talent.) Ben Jong himself seemed to understand our desire for flow, communication, and collaboration, and he demonstrated that in his concept. He got it!

As soon as he grasped the tight time frame, he brought in Team 7 International. Now, we had two architectural firms collaborating. In a typical buildout, the contractor is selected after designs and drawings are approved, so that bidding can proceed. Ben, however, insisted that the contractor be selected and awarded the business immediately. In addition to his reputation, the quality of his work, and his availability in the short time frame, the contractor had to have demonstrated collaborative skills.

The project was awarded to Rocky Moss at DPR, Inc. Rocky and his team began working immediately with our two architectural firms. They were able to input cost and time frame information into the design as it was developed. Even some design elements were suggested by the contractor, and construction improvements were suggested by the architects. Permits could be applied for as soon as pieces of the design were finalized, without even waiting for the finished project drawings.

On the agency side, we appointed a cross-functional team made up of people with good taste, a good feel for our culture, and strong collaborative skills. Vice presidents, junior art directors, and media supervisors worked side by side. Titles and hierarchy had no place in decision making. The representatives of the people who would actually use the space were empowered to make the decisions on just what the agency needed from both a functional and aesthetic perspective. This team made tough decisions, facing the critical issues of time, budget, and space allocation. Do we have showers for the runners or a playroom for the creatives? Do we make the conference room bigger and crowd three workspaces? Do we put in a focus group facility or another conference room? With the San Francisco approval cycle in the way, and some building structural issues affecting our desire to build a staircase to join our two floors, it was a little touch and go. We closed the old office on a Friday, right on schedule, and opened the new one on Monday.

What Was Different?

Collaboration

When we looked back at the two moves, we found some marked contrasts that begin to illustrate the new-age corporate behaviors. Our second, and more successful, move had a strong element of collaboration: Two architectural firms working with one another and with the contractor simultaneously. Our own people learned to collaborate with each other as well as with the three outside firms. Work that traditionally was done sequentially—finish the drawings, bid the job, hire the contractor, get the permits—was now being done concurrently.

Integration of Concept and Execution

In the first move, every group had a clearly defined function and there were sharp dividing lines between responsibilities. Now, the contractor was working hand in hand with the architects, the space planners, and our own teams, making design decisions, construction, and aesthetic decisions. The whole process was far more integrated and far more fluid. Very important, everyone worked not from a finished set of drawings, but from a concept statement—in a sense, a creative brief. Everyone clearly understood the design concept, which became the springboard for design decisions made on the fly.

Communication

The whole team met very frequently, often ad hoc, to discuss, recalibrate, and decide in real time. When we thought back on it, we realized that we had developed a substantially different work style over the last 10 years, mainly as a result of the kind of clients we were working with—fast-paced technology companies. The net result of the move was best summed up in the words of one of our staff members late Sunday afternoon after we had finished much of the unpacking: "This is so-o-o cool, I don't want to go home!"

Mastering Ambiguity

There was something else very special about the process. Without concrete plans and drawings for most of the four months and with decisions made literally on the fly, there was a certain ambiguity about the whole process, which is inherent in this kind of work style. This ambiguity might be difficult for many people who have grown up in structured environments with clear rules, boundaries, and expectations.

Empowerment

Our own people, the knowledge workers of our new economy, involved in this project felt exceptionally committed to the project. There was tremendous ownership of the results. The accountability for the results came not from management, but from the team members themselves. They felt that they could express their creativity at the same time they got an important job done. They enjoyed the hectic pace and doing several things at once, in which putting the puzzle together created a sense of discovery—just like some of the video games they grew up with. The constant communications made them feel like they were part of an important mission in which they were treated to all the information and the big picture, rather than the traditional need-to-know flow of information. Finally, although they all would say the project was grueling, they also all thought it was great fun! Go figure!

This is just one story, among many, about how four industries—architecture, design, construction, and advertising—mastered the new principles of collaboration, concurrent work, integration of disciplines, and fluidity. It is an indication of where the whole economy is moving. If nothing else, you should begin to see that it isn't just technology companies that have adopted these work styles, but many companies in many industries that are having to cope with the need for speed. Sequential, linear, hierarchical processes are going the way of the dinosaur, because they simply can no longer sustain competitive advantage.

6

New Tools to Help Warp-Speed Brand Builders

O bserving businesses, both corporate and agency, over the past few years, I've discovered that one of the most potent forces preventing marketing and advertising professionals from rethinking their brand strategies has been fear. They have tended to remain aloof from the advances in information technology, focusing more on the creative and human relations aspects of their business. As a result, they haven't always learned how to use technology in the context of building or maintaining brands.

There's a good reason for this. As we all know, the march of information technology into corporate life started in earnest in the 1980s. It began with automation of the paper-intensive portions of business. As business got bigger and more complex, it became impossible to track all the little numbers and bits and pieces of paper that every transaction generated. One of my summer jobs in college, I recall, was working in the credit department of Sears. The entire summer job consisted of filing little pink slips of paper, each one representing a charge transaction, into the file. Every morning, the 10 or so college students, hired to augment the regular staff at below-minimum wage, would get their pink stacks with a rubber band around them, and off we'd go to the racks of files for the rest of the day. The major challenge was to make sure we put the right slip into the file of the right John Smith on Cherry Street in Hayward. Our only diversion was an occasional incoming phone call for a credit check. When that phone rang, umpteen hands pounced on the receiver, each hoping they would be the first to break their personal monotony. It was this kind of drudgery that computers were first meant to help.

The first software programs were simply computerized versions of manual ways of doing things, and the hope was that it would be easier to retrieve numbers on a computer than it would to dig them out of dusty old file cabinets. In the early days of computing, I remember reading articles that computers didn't really increase productivity. Companies needed more people than before to input data and to manage their systems. The cost of the mainframe systems was exorbitant. The net, therefore, was that whatever time computers saved was offset by added costs. What a long time ago that seems now.

As systems improved, database technology evolved and networked systems became the norm, allowing information technology to reach many other sectors of corporate life. Wouldn't it be great to connect manufacturing into the database to keep track of parts and inventory? Wouldn't it be helpful to put shipping and order-processing information into the system? By now, most companies have expanded the network to help the sales department. Now, finally, in the late 1990s, information technology has dropped into the laps of marketing departments.

You have to understand technology to put it to good use. Unfortunately, technology illiteracy is not confined to the classrooms of America only. Currently, many marketing professionals prefer to leave technology to the techies, hoping they will somehow create new mechanisms to reach the customer. Even today, most corporate marketing departments still rely heavily on phones, faxes, and FedEx—even at sophisticated technology companies like Intel and Hewlett-Packard. It reminds me of the cobbler's children.

The barriers to literacy are everywhere. Many advertising agencies do not give their employees free access to the Internet. Even in technology-literate agencies, staffers sometimes find it hard to get the technology tools they need to do their jobs properly. TBWA/Chiat/Day, for instance, like many leading agencies, had great difficulty marrying creative and technology. Finally, management decided the agency couldn't execute web site development well, so it stopped trying. The Leo Burnett agency knew it needed to learn this field and, like many of its competitors, bought into a digital shop, Giant Step Productions. Giant Step's first mission was to conduct training sessions for Leo Burnett personnel so that they could better understand the new medium.

Technophobia or Lack of Tools?

The issue of technology literacy is an important one in two dimensions. One dimension is internal—the design of the flow of work in a warp-speed branding environment. Why does it take six months or more to develop an ad campaign when it takes only three months to develop a product? Time and time again, clients have come to us three months before launch with just a vague idea of the product, but with the expectation that the entire launch campaign can be ready in time. And, why can't it be?

The second dimension is external—how can technology literacy in the marketing and communications areas be leveraged to reach the consumer and build long-standing relationships with the brand? The problem with leaving this development to technologists is that they are focused on building systems, not on reaching the customer. Their experience base has been in the more routinized, process-oriented portions of corporate life. That experience is less suited to the fluid, hectic, creative-driven environments of ad agencies, corporate marketing departments, and other marketing communications agencies. Therefore, there really is no choice for agency chiefs like myself: Either embrace technology or cede business to people who do.

In our focus groups with marketing people, they express a latent fear of technology. It is not based on pure technophobia. These people surf the Net for information, buy their airline tickets online, and send electronic photos to their families. Rather, their fear is that somehow technology will impinge on their creativity and freedom. A computerized process is seen as mechanized, less free-flowing, less able to adapt to the spirit of invention. Their impressions seem to have been formed from the early days, when computers were not much fun to operate. They also suffer from a lack of appropriate tools—many of which are still under development. There is no question among marketing people that with the increased complexity of brand building in a global environment, and the pace of work, new tools would be helpful. To them, Microsoft Project is simply not the answer. Microsoft Project was built for engineers, Excel for accountants.

If the Right Tools Are the Answer, What's the Question?

How often we've heard the trite but true "Necessity is the mother of invention." That little phrase captures exactly why Winkler, an ad agency, developed TeamToolz, a sophisticated Web-based application designed to help clients manage the workflow of multiple agencies. TeamToolz was designed to foster communication and collaboration with the intent of helping brand builders integrate all the marketing communications of a brand. It has now proven to be able to help marketers keep track of all the intellec-

tual assets of brand communications—advertising, public relations, collateral, package design, event marketing, and so on—and
synchronize their work to get to market faster. If I said such a tool
could build strong bones, heal the sick, and help global companies
"think better," I would not be exaggerating by much.

It all started in February 1996. We were in the finals of a new
business pitch for a brand new printing supplies division of
Hewlett-Packard. Hewlett-Packard, fundamentally a hardware
company, had come to the recent realization that standard supplies for its printers (the replacement cartridges and the paper)
were a potentially bigger business in dollar volume than the printers themselves. The margin contribution could be greater too—a
case in which in the classic razor business model, blade sales out-
strip razor sales. Considering that every HP printer shipped with
an HP cartridge inside, an obvious objective would be to maintain
their 100 percent market share. Yet, printing supplies were receiving very little attention from HP, whereas competitors were beginning to launch campaigns for their own brands to work on HP
printers.

Clearly, it was past time for HP to concentrate on building its
own branded business. The 14 people from HP involved in making
the agency selection filed out of our conference room and
adjourned to a local bar for their final deliberations. HP has a very
highly evolved consensus management process, so that even one
dissenter can kill a vote. Imagine the whoop of excitement when
the call came—HP wanted to work with us. The assignment was
to be the lead agency over all the agencies in place.

This was to be a multiyear, long-term program for HP. New
skills sets were to be required. Though HP is an engineering-
driven company of the kind with which we were used to working,
this project called for advertising skills more typically required by
packaged-goods clients. Even the work style and culture of the
division would be different from the mother ship. People were
being recruited from other parts of HP and the outside, and there

were some 15 agency relationships that had been inherited from when supplies was a unit buried in the printer division. Then came the real challenge: The brand was to be launched officially in a scant six months, and it was to face a crowded field.

You can already see the threads of some of our earlier discussions about new-age work styles. Fast time to market, decentralized organization structure, the need to do work concurrently, and consensus decision making all came into play.

Our first challenge then was to combine what seemed on the surface to be two conflicting ways of doing business. On the one hand, HP had 15 agencies working on different aspects of brand communications for the printer supplies division. On the other hand, the client wanted a consensus-driven way to manage this decentralized structure. If we didn't have a mechanism to weave together all the different ideas, concepts, and executions from the 15 marketing suppliers, we would end up with a jumble. To build a clear and integrated brand, we had to also build a way for all the participants to communicate with each other throughout the process.

If you have lots of different agencies all adding to the mix, and lots of client approval levels, you'll only end up with an uncoordinated approach, which will frustrate the client and add to your workload. For us, an integrated approach from the get-go sounded like the best solution. However, getting over the typical turf battles when the client is organized around specialized marketing communications functions (direct mail, advertising, PR, collateral, channel marketing communications, trade shows, sports marketing, and so on) seemed to work against integration.

How to get all these talented people to work together when they all have different schedules, agendas, budgets, and approaches, and when they were all suspicious that all we were trying to do was steal part of their business, seemed an almost insurmountable barrier to success.

Low-Tech Brand Integration—Partnership Conferences

The first thing we proposed was to gather all the disparate agencies and client counterparts in one room. It was the first of several HP Partnership Conferences. Participating were representatives from Saatchi and Saatchi, Foote Cone Belding, the Evans Group, CKS, J. Brown and Partners, and Winkler Advertising, of course, to name just a few. The agenda for the first conference included an introduction to the research that HP had been conducting globally for the past year and a discussion with all the participants on its implications. Several of the companies had already begun work in their various disciplines. Packaging at that time had been almost finished, as it needed the longest lead time. Channel marketing programs were under way without being directed by any coherent brand strategy. It was clear to all of us at the meeting, agency and client alike, that there was good stuff underway, but none of it looked like it was emanating from a single brand.

For those of you who work with agencies, you are aware that putting agencies, used to dog-eat-dog competition for business and ideas, in a room was no small feat in itself. Add to that the fact that they would be sharing ideas in rough form before a group of their peers. Then, think about the politics of turfdom in corporate America. Each of the program managers, subbrand managers, and discipline specialists at HP also needed to share, communicate, and accept comments on what they were doing. To grease this human process, every conference included a significant social event designed just to let people get to know one another on a personal basis. One party, I recall, involved assigned teams after dinner that mixed up people from various agencies and client departments to guess the bands, songwriters, and singers of pieces of rock music from around the world. The teams bonded nicely—

so nicely, as a matter of fact, that it was slow going at the conference the following morning.

We supplemented the Partnership Conferences with the typical
fax, phone, e-mail, and trips on airplanes. When things are moving fast, however, you begin to realize that as much as you are communicating and sharing, just the days between FedEx deliveries
can cause confusion. A decision is made in the morning; it is communicated to some people that afternoon and to others in a week
when the next visit is scheduled. Still, others hear it by accident.
This causes lots of work to have to be redone in a complicated system, as everyone is just a little out of kilter, operating on information and decisions that have already been superceded. We clearly
had to find another way that would put everyone on the same page
in real time and allow all concerned to continue updating and
commenting on new developments as deadlines were met and
decisions were made.

High-Tech Tools for Brand Integration

Winkler has developed numerous tools for brand integration, any
of which you might find useful for your own business.

The Client Private Office™

While we were mulling over all this, we realized we had just posted
a creative brief to the Client Private Office for Hewlett-Packard.
This is our name for a private, secure web site set up for each of our
clients, accessible only with a password. We routinely posted all
current work in progress, including briefs, current research results,
timelines, estimates, even layouts and copy, and final work to
these internal web sites. Clients had the ability to view work at
any hour of the day and night. When they were traveling, which
was often, this was sometimes the only way work on deadline
could be presented and approved. As a result, deadlines were met.

Even here, though, we decided our standard Client Private Office didn't meet the needs of Hewlett-Packard, and we took the idea a step further.

Virtual Account Planning Panel™

The idea for this more sophisticated international tool grew out of our implementation of a global brand strategy for another client, Ascend. The company made remote networking products that let users dial up from anywhere around the world. The company's equipment helped make the Internet possible, so it's no accident that we used the Internet to solve the brand-building problem for them. Imagine that you have an account that has to reach around the world. It's a global assignment, but you have been given neither a global budget nor enough time to get the job done properly. The solution? After you reach for the Advil, you start to think about the technology you have available to see if there is a creative way to solve the problem.

Our answer was something we called the Virtual Account Planning Panel. Account planning, as you recall, is a relatively new advertising discipline that draws insights into the advertising strategy from consumer behavior. Before you solve a brand problem, you need to know how consumers relate to the brand and its competitors. In the past, advertisers and their agencies relied on raw research data or focus groups. Now there is an effort to have trained specialists do this kind of work using more subjective techniques. As a result, they are able to answer such questions as: What does the product or service stand for? How will people respond to a new brand position or brand message? Are the attitudes toward the brand different in different parts of the world? What experiences have consumers had with other products that offered similar new benefits?

The Virtual Account Planning Panel was essentially an intranet we developed to help us get such consumer insights quickly from around the world. As a small agency with only one office in San Francisco, we had to create global reach without bricks and mortar. We had to be creative to do it. Once again, we harnessed the power of technology. We recruited 20 freelance planners around the world, and set them up with passwords on our Intranet. Through this vehicle, we could communicate with them at any time of day, without having materials hung up in customs. We could post a brief on the virtual planning panel and get a response in 48 hours or less—a saving of weeks compared with other methods. Planners from different parts of the world could see the responses we were getting from other members of the panel and communicate with each other, increasing their own knowledge base. Our work could be checked in real time, at tissue stage. So we knew right away if a concept we were developing for one client in one country would work globally. Our planners were thrilled to be working with us breaking new ground with planning and technology, and our clients were thrilled with the speed and reach we developed.

For Adaptec, a Silicon Valley company specializing in input and output devices for computers, our Virtual Account Planning Panel told us that an ad we had developed using a graphic of the Volkswagen Beetle, to signify simple and utilitarian in the United States, didn't have that same meaning in Germany. In Germany, the Volkswagen Beetle stood for a cheap, poorly made car.

We changed the concept and averted a major blunder. For LSI Logic, a concept based on getting to market faster with LSI's ASIC chip sets, using a surreal visual of a clock wasn't clear the way we conceived it, because the French had a different perception about time than Americans have. We had the opportunity to make the change before we even presented *the idea* to the client.

TeamToolz

In the case of Hewlett-Packard's printing supplies, we decided to take these two ideas—The Client Private Office and The Virtual Account Planning Panel—and develop a significantly more sophisticated tool. This application was truly a marriage of advertising and technology—and I mean this in the most literal of ways. Our director of account planning at the time was Nina Milosevic, a very intelligent dynamic character from Serbia who spoke several languages and gave our global account planning an international flavor. She was married to our chief technology officer, Voja Lalich, who was a brilliant technical person, particularly in this emerging area of web-based applications. Voja had spent enough time around Nina to begin to understand the craziness of advertising and brand building, and Nina knew how to articulate the issues and intrigue him into thinking about new solutions. We at Winkler and our clients were the beneficiaries.

Add to that the fact that we had a visionary client, Daina Middleton, the brand manager at HP printer supplies, and we had the basic ensemble to come up with a unique and powerful solution. As a result, TeamToolz was born—a technology tool built by marketing people for marketing people.

Standard TeamToolz home page.

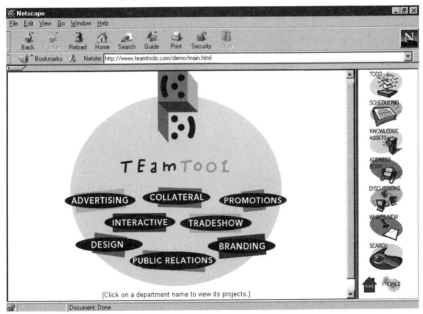

The key was to come up with a product that would mirror the way individuals work together at a "Partners Conference" and in real-time situations. First, we needed a better understanding of those processes. We hired a project manager to do a needs analysis. With input from HP and from all the partner agencies, we finally felt confident that we had the information needed to guide the technical people in their development. Our account management folks regularly talked with our technical folks as well as with the clients as the project developed. Then we hired Sage Solutions, a Silicon Valley–based systems design and software development house to actually build the first version of the application. We then allowed TeamToolz to be spun out as its own company to avoid single-agency or -client ties.

The frustrations and struggles that we constantly heard about from both the client and the agency sides focused heavily on four areas:

1. *Trouble with effective coordination:* Few companies had any mechanisms for coordinating the various communications disciplines within their companies, much less coordinating the work of outside agencies.
2. *Problems with project management:* Especially in a fast environment in which there was no time for checks and rechecks.
3. *Frustrations with communication:* Someone always felt out of the loop on some critical piece of information, which caused wasted time and money as stuff had to be scrapped and redone.
4. *Storage of the materials:* It seemed nothing essential was ever handy or even easy to find, especially when you were in a hurry.

All four of these buckets of daily Excedrin headaches often led to poor brand integration, lower quality of work, and higher costs, as the wheel had to be reinvented because the artwork, the logo, or the media schedule was misplaced.

Time for the Cavalry

The challenge was then to translate these struggles and frustrations into a software application that answered these four needs. We built a project management tool for each of the marketing communications disciplines with project milestones, which users could define with a simple point and click.

We added communications capabilities to keep everyone in the loop and automatic e-mail notification to prompt people when they needed to do something to move the project along. We included ways to upload and store any kind of digital file that was important to the brand—from competitive marketing information to strategic documents to finished ads to commercials. Uploading is as easy as putting an enclosure into an e-mail.

We added a common area so that everyone in the system would have the ability to access finished work, logos, artwork, trademark

Project management web page.

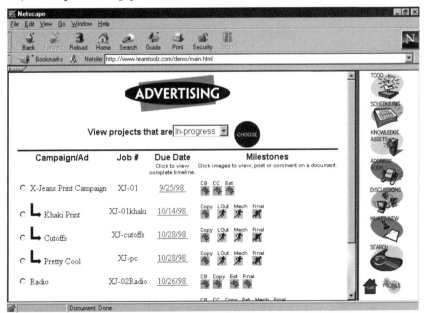

Screen shot of personal to-do list.

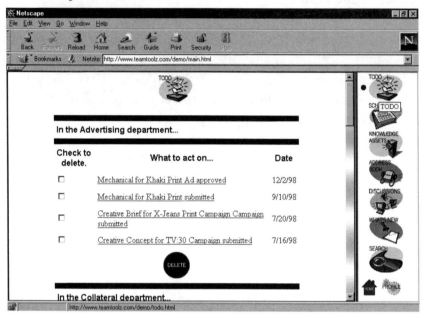

information, and all of the sundry bits and pieces of information that constantly get lost or misplaced, but which people throughout the vast marketing team network need to have. The Tool Box within TeamToolz contains brand guidelines, logos, line art, trademark guidelines, as well as specific images that have been approved with usage requirements. In this way, we are all working from the same set of blueprints but are encouraged to make use of our different perspectives. Finally, the shared intelligence, or "war room," area in TeamToolz holds the most current competitive information in reports, articles, speeches, even tidbits from the salespeople in the field.

The system has a powerful database behind it so that all the intellectual property of the brand can be stored in one place and available to anyone with approved access. Because TeamToolz was designed to mirror the way people work, it was created with so-called departments, so that each agency also has its own area to exchange work in progress with the corresponding client. The brand manager, or supraclient, has the ability to have a bird's-eye view of all of this activity, and of course, also has the ability to reorder priorities if things seemed to be going awry.

TeamToolz has other attributes. For one, we tried to take in the human dynamic of working together; therefore, we also created an address book. The address book contains the standard address information about people working on the account at all the agencies and levels. It also includes a digital photo to give the system life. You can see to whom you are sending a message, and you can sort by name, agency, or photo, if you met someone but can't remember his or her name. Taking advantage of the Internet's newsgroup functions, we created an electronic bulletin board, which allows users to post topics for discussion and leave comments for review.

Here again, we were mindful that not all of us would be in the office at the same time, nor would we even be in the same time zone. Instead of viewing this as an obstacle to creative collaboration, we used technology to solve the problem. Both the HP clients and its agencies found that TeamToolz supported existing processes and improved communications by allowing internal and external advertising and marketing teams to be more productive.

Communications were improved and frustrations decreased as delays in approval cycles were shortened. All involved experienced a reduction in the cost of FedEx and spent less time copying and faxing. Putting TeamToolz in place allowed us to get away from the excuses and closer to action. The refrain, "Oh, just fax that media plan to me again," was heard less often, because the client could access it easily enough him- or herself. No more dashing to the FedEx office by 5:30 P.M. for East Coast pickup, when we would have really liked another hour to go over the comps to make sure they were right. Because many reviews and approvals were being done electronically, there were fewer out-of-town trips, thereby reducing travel wear and tear and costs.

Ultimately, the work began to have a more integrated look and feel as agencies had the opportunity to see each others' pieces even before they hit the media. Because some of the time normally spent on coordination and reduction of confusion could now be spent on the work, the quality of the work began to improve slowly.

For the brand manager, TeamToolz is about facilitating brand integration. TeamToolz software is designed to make the brand manager's job easier, locally and globally. It allows for more seamless marketing communications. The brand manager has at his or her fingertips all project status reports and calendars on marketing activities, assigned responsibilities, automated progress updates, and deadline warnings. The real beauty of TeamToolz, however, is the way it integrates text, data, graphics, and video.

Want to see the last cut of the commercial? No problem, it's just a click away. All of the brand manager's agency resources are available any time of night or day and anywhere the brand manager is as long as he or she has access to any PC or Mac browser and the Internet. The program also has complete archiving capabilities for all marketing communications. This allows the brand manager more time to think about knowledge management rather than just process—something that, until now, has been elusive when the job is trying to coordinate vast numbers of people toward a common goal.

Version 1.0 of TeamToolz was deployed at Hewlett-Packard in May of 1997. Since then, it has gone through several revisions and enhancements. The current version 2.1 is a richer and simpler-to-use product. Because HP is a technology company, it may have been easier for them to see the advantages of TeamToolz; for another client, CyberStar, a provider of broadband communications services in the Loral family of companies, the results were even more obvious. Implemented and trained in December of 1997, seven agencies went to work on a major launch program, which was to be kicked off at the National Association of Broadcasters (NAB) show in March, just three months later. With the help of this coordinating technology, the company was assured the trade show booth would be designed and built on time, the booth video and live show produced, the collateral printed, the print and TV ad campaign on the air, all with some semblance of continuity of message, theme, and style.

TeamToolz is one of those small revolutions in the process of the development of work that is essentially intellectual property. TeamToolz has tried to make it responsive to the way agencies and clients really work. The development of TeamToolz led us to go a long way toward overcoming the barriers to a truly integrated brand. It has done so by reducing the problems of coordinating different agencies with different specialties. Until now, if a client wanted an integrated strategy and execution, the only solution was to get one agency. Even then, most found that it was a solution fraught with difficulty. Any big agency holding company is just that. Every specialty and every local agency is a separate profit center, and there is generally very little communication, much less true coordination of services—not unlike the friction, turfdom, and politics inside the client's own organization as everyone competes for resources, attention, and glory. Because agency talents are uneven and there are a variety of vested interests in the global client and the global agency, brand integration usually falls by the wayside. Yet, as technology creates multiple points of contact with the consumer, it becomes even more important to focus on the integration of disciplines, messages, and programs—not just for the sake of efficiency, but for the sake of effectiveness.

Now, for the first time, with a tool like TeamToolz, it is possible to actually consider hiring agencies that are truly the best in their respective fields, even if they are not part of the same big agency network, and they can now have their work coordinated in a way that was unthinkable before. Now, by using TeamToolz, collaboration rather than confrontation can define the inter- and intra-agency relationship. Decentralized decision making is no longer a hallmark of loose management, but is an ingredient in creating a dynamic brand strategy, managed through technology.

7

The Brand Ecosystem

In a very simple way, marketers have long known that relationships with other brands affect their own brand. You won't find Ralph Lauren clothes at Sears, for instance, because the brand of the retailer is not complementary to the manufacturer's brand. Department store cosmetics like Estée Lauder and Lancôme won't occupy shelf space in the cosmetic departments of drugstores, nor will Maybelline have a counter at Macy's for the same reason. However, you did find *Jurassic Park* cups at McDonald's, because the appeal of a blockbuster movie with mass appeal ties in very well with a mass-appeal food chain. American Express Platinum Card has hooked up with high-end luxury hotels and resorts to provide special amenities, such as room upgrades, free breakfasts, and four o'clock tea, to Platinum Card customers. Benetton, in fact, is thinking of producing a low-end line of clothing through Sears—just as Martha Stewart Living has a line of towels and linens at Kmart, because these brands want to mix their appeal with the retailers' reach.

In technology, however, nothing is simple, even brand relationships. Let's take a good look at what I've learned from observing technology companies and what happens to brand relationships.

Throughout almost my entire career, the launch of a new brand was discussed in terms of its identity from the point of view of the "financial owner" of the brand. Companies wanting to launch products or services traditionally enlisted the help of the advertising agency to produce advertising and perhaps a logo or a package design—some sort of physical branding—to supplement the personality or character of the brand that has been determined as the best choice by the company. The thinking in the old paradigm believed the brand belonged primarily to the company that owned and launched it, and, often times, it personified the character of the manufacturer. BMW is an engineering company, and the brand stands for solid engineering with an aura of exclusiveness coming from both its high-performance characteristics as well as its price tag. Ben & Jerry's Ice Cream, for example, reflects the funky, quirky nature of its founders, and it mirrors that personality in the brand with crazy flavors like "Cherry Garcia" and "Phish Food," and interesting decor in the stores themselves.

Another approach to crafting the personality or character was influenced heavily by what research said consumers would respond to. Cheer Detergent built a strong brand around "All-Tempa-Cheer," which came out of consumer research showing that consumers were confused about what temperatures were best for what kinds of garments and what colors could be washed together. How about Dawn Dishwashing Liquid, which was positioned to solve the biggest perceived problem of washing dishes by hand—the grease that seems to be everywhere in the water and on the dishes? In these cases, the brand strategy was crafted around the intersection of what the product or service did and what the consumer wanted to hear.

Sometimes, the brand personality has been crafted with the competition in mind. I recently had the opportunity to work with one of the global advertising agencies on a telecommunications launch. The brand strategy was crafted solely in terms of a positioning against a major competitor and was defined in terms of its personality relative to the competitor—approachable and likeable, with a touch of irreverence. In this case, neither the consumer, nor the company in question, were much of a factor in the strategy.

Some marketers prefer to talk in terms of brand promise first, and then deal with the issues of personality and character later. When this approach is used, the brand is crafted as a singular promise that can be delivered on forever and can transcend different campaigns and varying permutations of business strategy. When Chevy's, a Mexican restaurant chain (originally owned by PepsiCo and spun off in 1997) launched its first advertising campaign, it used the brand promise of fresh Mexican food. The tag line on the award-winning campaign developed by Goodby Silverstein and Partners in San Francisco was "Fresh Mex." The original campaign was also fresh, in that commercials were developed daily with man-on-the-street interviews edited and on air the very next day. We were all amazed when, every day on our TVs in the San Francisco Bay Area, we saw a new spot. This was before all the computerized digital editing equipment was as available as it is today. This clever approach emphasized the major product/service benefit of freshness. Whereas consumer desire for fresh food informed the brand promise, the roots of the brand and its definition were squarely in the hands of the owner. Similarly, Southwest Airlines pioneered a concept that has now become a category—the low-cost airline. Their brand promise embodies cheap, dependable air travel with a sense of fun. Again, the owner of the brand is clear, and the definition comes inherently from the service itself. The company providing the service drove the definition of the brand.

Most marketers will be quick to acknowledge that, over time, the consumer adds his or her own attitudes and belief systems to the brand mystique. Coca-Cola started out as a drink—brown sugared water—and has become over the years a global symbol of the American lifestyle. That happened partially through the advertising and marketing activities of the Coca-Cola Company and partially through American GIs, first, and then the backpacking and jet-setting crowds of American tourists spreading American culture and lifestyles around the globe. Arm & Hammer Baking Soda, a venerable old brand, started out as a cooking ingredient. Then, consumers started to brush their teeth with it and stick open boxes of it into refrigerators and freezers to absorb odors. This has led to all kinds of brand extensions into carpet cleaners, deodorizers, and underarm deodorants. In these examples, the brands became an interesting combination of company and consumer.

Now, all of this is about to change. The world of brands, owned and controlled by the many manufacturers, is a fading world. The schematic I dug out of the agency's historical files that shows the branding system as it was practiced some 20 years ago—and is still practiced today by some very traditional, not very "Warp Speed"–thinking companies, shows how linear and organized our thinking was.

It's No Longer a Stand-Alone World

Now, take a look at how a technology company approaches a product launch today. In this industry, a new product is often created as the result of alliances, partnerships, and various forms of technical dependencies in a very big way, and thus the brand torch has to reflect this interdependence. Think for a moment about your computer. It's not actually one product; rather, it's a collection of subsystems, each of which is produced by a different industry: The displays industry makes the monitor; the storage industry makes the drives; the semiconductor industry makes the chips; and the software industry makes the operating systems and the applications software. Some analysts would even subdivide the software industry

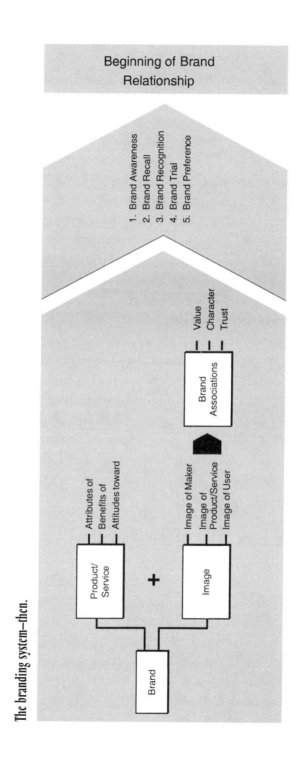

The branding system—then.

147

into categories like databases, applications software, utilities, operating software, middleware, and so forth. The list goes on.

Now, complicate this picture by saying that all of these subsystems, which can be assembled in multiple ways, have to talk to each other. No wonder the industry has a reputation for "plug and pray." It's easy to see why, in a complicated environment like this, there have to be strategic alliances, consortia, and self-created standards bodies to try to make everything work together. Henry Ford's early days of, "You can have a car in any color as long as it is black," are long over. So are the days of the one phone call to the one phone company for installation or repair.

Today, technology companies who are in fierce competition with each other in the marketplace are also inking joint development agreements, sharing software code, and divulging product road maps to each other because they have to. This really has an effect on brand. Does the Hewlett-Packard brand suffer if the Intel chips in its products are flawed? Does the Intel brand suffer if Compaq produces a slow computer? Without a doubt. That's the double-edged sword of the Intel Inside campaign, in which you have much-publicized outside partners whose product and services influence each other, and hence, the whole brand relationship.

So, What the Heck Is the Brand Ecosystem?

In a nutshell, it's the increasingly complex set of interrelationships of all of the stakeholders and brands involved in putting together a product or a service. In the examples we just talked about in the beginning of this chapter, the brand relationships are small in number and as such, are not so difficult to manage. Take a typical software product, however. The application probably has to be Microsoft Windows–compatible. It has to be able to run on all computer brands, and the box will usually specify which Pentium processors have enough power to run the application. Now, add

Pentium and Intel to the brand effect. We already have five brands involved, and we haven't yet begun to think about distribution or promotion. Every brand with which our brand allies has an impact on the brand. That's why I have found it useful to start thinking much more broadly when facing branding decisions, and begin to consider something I call "The Brand Ecosystem."

A Complex Organism

This Brand Ecosystem manifests itself and affects brand decisions in many ways. The stakeholders in a Brand Ecosystem are getting more numerous. It is not enough anymore to think just about the consumer and the competition when making brand decisions. Although technology companies have been at the forefront of dealing with ever more complex Brand Ecosystems, this situation is no longer one faced exclusively by technology companies. I sit on the board of Lifeguard, a premier regional HMO in California. This company's stakeholders are many. First, there are the employees who select Lifeguard as their health insurer. An important additional constituency are the families of the employees, who are also consumers of the service. Then, there are the employers, who decide which HMO the company will provide and foot the majority of the bill, and certainly they are major stakeholders. Then, there are the employees of Lifeguard, who process the claims and make decisions regarding what will and won't be covered and when payments will be sent, who also are stakeholders.

Less obvious, but just as important in the Brand Ecosystem stakeholders organization chart of an HMO, are the people and organizations who actually deliver the service, the independent doctors who sign up with Lifeguard to provide medical care—and with them, their clinics, nurses, receptionists, lab staff, and so on. Then, we have to count the hospitals with which the doctors are affiliated. Of course, we cannot forget the state insurance commis-

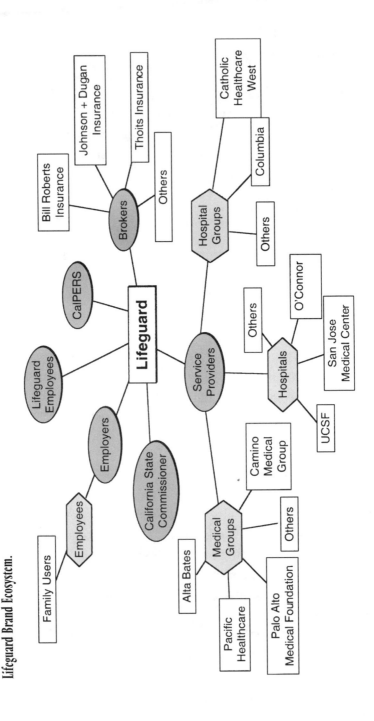

Lifeguard Brand Ecosystem.

sioners, who can affect what Lifeguard can and cannot do. Major customers such as the California Public Employees' Retirement System (PERS) will have a significant effect on the Lifeguard brand, based on how it perceives Lifeguard service. PERS will also impact Lifeguard by what new products or services it will demand in the future, and even whether it continues to do business with Lifeguard. Because of the size of its "covered lives," the number of people on the California state payroll, PERS carries clout in the industry far beyond its own contracts. We cannot forget brokers either, who represent the sales and distribution systems.

If we count the classes of stakeholders and the brands involved, it's easy to realize that the Brand Ecosystem gets harder and harder to chart, much less manage or control. Aside from the large number of stakeholders, there are multiple brands that deliver the service, directly impacting Lifeguard's brand. The clinics and doctors' groups with which Lifeguard contracts to treat patients have a lot to do with how Lifeguard is perceived, yet Lifeguard has little control over what happens to a patient there. Hospitals have been creating their own brands for some time, and they are part of the health care and Brand Ecosystem for Lifeguard, yet the main influence Lifeguard can have over them is through payment policies. Of course, the employer's health care policies at work also affect the Lifeguard brand.

In technology, as well as in other fields, *products and services are increasingly delivered as a combination*. Dine-One-One and Waiters on Wheels co-opt with restaurants to give the consumer an efficient home delivery system and a wide range of restaurant choices. The consumer experience is a blend of the two brands. Similarly, for years, the car industry has been selling through a network of independent, but licensed, dealers. Consumers have been giving the dealers a bad rap. Buying a car has been termed one of the worst experiences a consumer can have—very close to having your teeth drilled. Understanding the impact of the dealer experience on the car brand, Saturn chose to create its own totally new dealer network to solve the problem, and to rely on those dealers to reinforce the Saturn brand through the experience they deliver to the car buyer.

A Dynamically Changing Organism

In addition to greater complexity, the Brand Ecosystem has another dynamic at work—constant change. A well-known example in the technology business is what happened to Hayes modems. At the beginning of the personal computer revolution, Hayes modems were practically the only modem of choice. Founded in 1978, Hayes Microcomputer produced modems that were compatible with computers that were made mostly from kits. When IBM launched the first PC back in 1981, Hayes was right there supplying modems to the growing audience of computer users; however, Hayes didn't keep pace with changing manufacturing and distribution. Mail-order competition and lower-priced modems flooded the market. Management turmoil and fierce competition forced the company into bankruptcy in 1994. The Hayes brand, however, was still valid enough to lure takeover attempts by US Robotics and Diamond Multimedia in 1996—two years after bankruptcy! Hayes ended up selling half the company to an Asian consortium and the brand lives on mostly in memory, a footnote in the technology revolution. Still, it offers important brand lessons.

Here was a brand that had captured the market in an ecosystem that changed dramatically in the 15 years since the first PC. The company failed to recognize signs that the technology industry was changing to encompass faster, internal modems. It stopped being identified as a player or a leader in an ecosystem that prizes innovation above all else.

A more successful example is Creative Labs. Initially, this U.S. subsidiary of a Singapore-based enterprise was to provide engineering services for hire and make clones of Apple and PC computers for the Asian market. Because of increased competition in the personal computer market, however, the company shifted direction and decided to make sound cards and other add-on features used in computers. In 1989, Creative Labs introduced the Sound Blaster card, which became an industry standard as well as a recognized brand. As computers grew in power and users demanded more multimedia products, Creative made deals with the computer makers to supply boards that would be installed inside the machines. Compaq and Dell gave even more legitimacy to Creative's products. Despite greater competition in the add-on market, Creative continued to introduce new technology to enhance the performance of personal computers. Fax programs and graphics accelerator cards were created. The company even formed an alliance with Samsung, in which the Korean electronics giant would make Creative's CD-ROM drive products.

Through intelligent management of product development and alliances with industry leaders, such as Hewlett-Packard, NEC, IBM, Gateway 2000, and Intel, Creative Labs has managed to survive in a cutthroat industry. It has created a brand with its Sound Blaster cards that still stands for high quality and up-to-date technology.

Other industries have begun to face Brand Ecosystem issues as well. UAL, owners of United Airlines, the world's biggest air carrier, has taken code sharing to a new level. Code sharing is an airline practice designed to help regional and national carriers extend their service by partnering with other airlines in the geographies they do not serve.

United has a code-sharing agreement with more than a dozen other airlines and has even put considerable energy and money into branding the agreements. The Star Alliance, formed in 1997, brings together Lufthansa, Scandinavian Airlines Systems, Air Canada, Thai International, Varig, and United for a global operation that goes beyond a fancy new logo. The companies share revenue on some routes, operate joint ticket offices, and also make joint purchases. Of course, the passenger also gets the benefits of using frequent flier miles interchangeably. The Brand Ecosystem for both United and the traveler has just gotten more complex.

Just as we agreed that consumers impact brands by giving them a life of their own, so do all the stakeholders in the brand. As the brand becomes defined in much broader terms by suppliers, partners, customers, strategic allies, development partners, and investors, the way we think about the brand has to encompass a whole new structure, a Brand Ecosystem that has a life of its own. Multiple constituencies complicate the brand definition. Furthermore, as we discussed in earlier chapters, new technologies like the Internet change the linear movement from brand awareness through preference to a concurrent jumble, different in almost every situation. I've had to redraw our brand schematic to reflect the new reality. Take a look at then and now as shown on pages 156–157.

What Can You Do?

Other than give up because the situation is much too difficult, my experience suggests five concrete actions or programs you can undertake to be more successful in building your own Brand Ecosystem on a strong, viable foundation.

1. *Identify all the stakeholders of your brand and begin charting the Ecosystem relationships.* As a first step, consider performing a brand audit, or at least an assessment. Chapter 9 will give you a road map to implement a successful brand assessment in this changed environment. Your next step, and one you should undertake whether you do anything else, should be to conduct a rigorous process to identify all the stakeholders and other brands involved in your Brand Ecosystem, using a guide like the one I've developed, which follows. I think you'll be surprised by what you find. You'll need to consult not just the marketing department and your product-

marketing people, but also your sales organization to see if there is any cross-selling or informal product bundling going on, your business development people who are out cutting various deals, your finance people who may be involved in merger-and-acquisition discussions, your manufacturing people who are likely putting together master vendor programs and making special arrangements to improve manufacturing cycle times, and your research and development folks who may have joint development programs or licensing deals going on.

You'll want to prioritize the importance of each of these stakeholders in your Brand Ecosystem so that you'll be sure about the critical points to watch most closely. Finally, you'll want to establish a process to capture additions to the Brand Ecosystem as they occur. Just like the ecosystem of nature, the Brand Ecosystem is dynamic and is affected by environmental changes and must be monitored periodically.

2. *Appoint a Brand Ecosystem steward to monitor changes in the composition of the system.* Congratulations, if you've finished step 1. Before you get too pleased with yourself, however, remember that a Brand Ecosystem is a dynamic environment that is always changing—either growing or withering depending on your management of the ecosystem. You are in the best position to track this dynamic, so it is important that you occasionally rechart the system to keep up with changes taking place. If you are in a fast-moving industry, your whole landscape could change in a single quarter. To stay on top of this, it is important to appoint someone to be responsible for the process of reviewing changes on your brand identifier list, as well as industry changes that might make you want to proactively consider forcing some alterations in your brand relationships. If you keep to this process, I promise you will be better informed for making good branding decisions. You will also make better strategic decisions for your business.

3. *Clearly articulate your brand strategy—in writing.* My guess is that the brand list you produced is longer than you originally

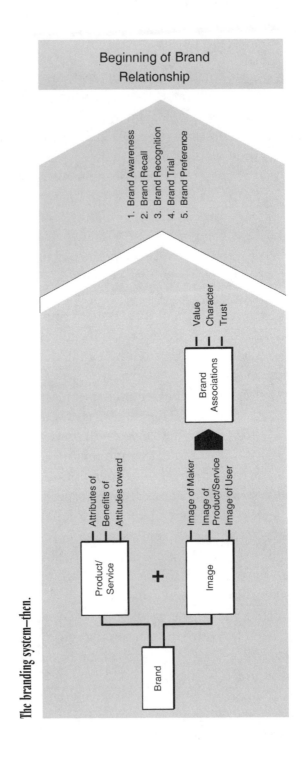

The branding system—then.

The branding system—now.

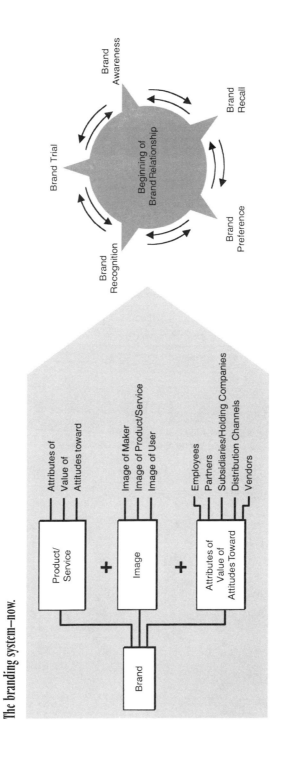

Brand Ecosystem Identifier

Fill in each stakeholder in your Brand Ecosystem by interviewing each department responsible for the relationships or searching through your corporate databases. Rank each stakeholder class on a scale of 1 to 5, with 5 for those stakeholders who are critical influencers and 1 for those stakeholders who are minimal influencers.

Stakeholder

Rank						Rank				
Low				High		Low				High
Financial	1	2	3	4	5	**Customers**	1	2	3	4	5
• Shareholders	O—O—O—O—O					• Current Customers	O—O—O—O—O
• Investment Partners	O—O—O—O—O					• Prospects	O—O—O—O—O
• Financial Analysts	O—O—O—O—O					• Competitive Customers	O—O—O—O—O
▪	O—O—O—O—O					▪	O—O—O—O—O
▪	O—O—O—O—O					▪	O—O—O—O—O
▪	O—O—O—O—O					▪	O—O—O—O—O

Your Organization		**Decision Influences**	
• Employees	O—O—O—O—O	• Industry Influencers	O—O—O—O—O
• Subsidiary Companies	O—O—O—O—O	• Market Analysts	O—O—O—O—O
• Holding Companies	O—O—O—O—O	• Industry Associations	O—O—O—O—O
▪	O—O—O—O—O	▪	O—O—O—O—O
▪	O—O—O—O—O	▪	O—O—O—O—O
▪	O—O—O—O—O	▪	O—O—O—O—O

Distribution Channels		**Strategic Partners**	
• Wholesalers	O—O—O—O—O	• Joint Marketing Partners	O—O—O—O—O
• Dealers	O—O—O—O—O	• Alliance Partners	O—O—O—O—O
• Retailers	O—O—O—O—O	• Development Partners	O—O—O—O—O
• Mass Merchants	O—O—O—O—O	• Key Vendors	O—O—O—O—O
• OEMs	O—O—O—O—O	▪	O—O—O—O—O
• Catalog Resellers	O—O—O—O—O	▪	O—O—O—O—O
• E-Commerce Resellers	O—O—O—O—O		
▪	O—O—O—O—O		
▪	O—O—O—O—O		
▪	O—O—O—O—O		

List all 5-point Stakeholders	List all 4-point Stakeholders
————————	————————
————————	————————
————————	————————

(your most important brand audiences)

```
┌─────────────────────────────────────────────┐
│        Appointed Brand Ecosystem Steward     │
│                                              │
│         _____          │
│                    Name                      │
│   Title _____        │
│                                              │
│                                              │
│   Phone _____ E-mail _____    │
│                                              │
│   Date of next scheduled review_____   │
└─────────────────────────────────────────────┘
```

anticipated. If that's the case, doesn't it stand to reason that your brand strategy should be shared with those stakeholders who have the greatest impact on your brand? How can you share it if it isn't well defined in the first place? In my experience, many companies rely on a campaign platform originally intended to drive their advertising, and once that is developed and approved, simply forget to follow through. At best, they rely on the intuitive abilities of the agencies to reverse-engineer the brand strategy from past decisions. This is not the best way to get your brand equity dollars to increase, and it certainly is no longer possible to do in a complex Brand Ecosystem. Your brand strategy, brand promise, brand essence, character and personality should be well thought out and articulated in writing, so that it can be passed on to all of the stakeholders. That's the only way to keep your brand from becoming diluted by the impact of all its other brand relationships. Your brand will grow and change as it adapts to its environment, but your job is to make sure that it continues to be strong and healthy.

4. *Implement a brand strategy communications program for the entire Brand Ecosystem.* Now that you've decided to focus on the Brand Ecosystem, and you have developed the strategy statement, make sure you have a mechanism in place to inform all your stakeholders who influence the brand, not just your marketing people

and the agencies. Also, make sure that you have a mechanism in place to keep reinforcing the message. This should demand the same level of attention as promulgating the corporate objectives. Everyone involved in the system should be able to tell you what your brand promise is. If they cannot, how can they make decisions that will affect the brand positively as opposed to negatively?

When we did a brand assessment for Tektronix, part of the program included a whole communications plan developed to inform and excite all the stakeholders in the brand. There was as much creativity in this program as in the advertising campaign that we proposed! Globalstar, the new satellite global telephone service, has structured a multiyear communications program to touch all of the Globalstar-brand constituencies, starting with equity investors, equipment manufacturers, and service providers (many of whom were the same organizations). Worldwide local providers in 100-plus countries were next, and Globalstar developed a global advertising program to support sales and operations programs with these providers well before consumer service would actually be available. Then, with critical input from Globalstar's on-the-ground partners throughout the world, to reflect the truly global nature of the business, branding programs to influence target consumers were built on the foundation that began with the industry infrastructure several years earlier.

5. *Make your brand strategy part of all your alliance contracts and agreements.* It is interesting to me how often in contract negotiations for joint programs, projects, or alliances, brand issues are simply not on the table. It is particularly mystifying when these brand issues can involve millions or even billions of dollars of shareholder equity, when powerful brands are joining forces. It's essential to look at both the branding opportunities and problems that such alliances will generate, and take a tip from companies like Intel, whose clear vision of the Intel brand and where it was heading played a vital role in structuring the well-known and highly successful Intel Inside program, or follow the example of Netscape.

Early in its history, Netscape recognized the value of branding and implemented a program called "Netscape Now," which became part of every contract. Basically, anyone can feature a Netscape Now button on their web site—with text explaining its usage. For web sites optimized for Netscape Communication, the recommended text is: "This site is best viewed with Netscape Communicator. Download Netscape Now!" When someone clicks on the button they are automatically routed back to the Netscape site so they can download the current version of Netscape Communicator.

Why Aren't We All Doing This Already?

How do you coordinate action with all the vendors, partners, and other stakeholders who are vital to the health of your Brand Ecosystem? Some people achieve the appropriate level of orchestration through corporate mission statements that may embody the brand promise, with both inside and outside groups required to understand and implement it in their own programs. Chances are good that your own organization has such a mission statement, but ask yourself whether it will provide the direction needed, both internally and with the expanding parts of your Brand Ecosystem.

Others rely on their advertising agency to function as the brand steward. As a matter of fact, that is the positioning of Ogilvy and Mather, the agency for notable brands such as IBM, American Express, and Jaguar. Relying on the agency, however, is getting increasingly difficult for two reasons. One is, of course, the increasing complexity of the Brand Ecosystem, involving parts of the organization and outside influences that agencies typically don't touch. The other is the trend to move agency relationships out of the executive suite and into the bowels of marketing communications.

When the job of branding becomes a functional activity with little authority to cross over into other functions, it becomes almost impossible to leverage the extraordinary financial power of the brand. As ad agencies have been relegated to a more marginal role in the management of the brand, a vacuum has been created, which now is being filled by the new brand consultancies. These consultants are often invited into higher levels of the corporation where their analytical approaches to problem definition and modeling of solutions are readily understood and appreciated by senior management. These consultants can be very valuable in bringing attention to the issue and in establishing the processes to manage the Brand Ecosystem.

The Brand Needs a Soul

What these consultants cannot do is create soul for the brand. In the end, the brand needs a creative expression, and that creative expression is as much about the human condition as it is about the facts of the product or the industry. Advertising people and other communications professionals have an enormous opportunity in the Brand Ecosystem because, of all corporate constituencies, they know how to harness the combined power of emotion and logic. They are able to craft this combination into powerful communications that can create that coveted relationship with the consumer and with all of the stakeholders of the Brand Ecosystem—the brand relationship.

8

Warp-Speed Branding and the Internet: How It Relates to the New Marketing Reality

To stay ahead of the curve in the new marketing environment, everyone in the marketing process is going to have to ensure that they are comfortable with technology and its strategic applications. It is not enough to subscribe to computer magazines or read the technology sections of mainstream business publications. Marketing professionals have got to get their hands dirty and start applying some of the technology consumers understand and employ.

Consumers are often far more advanced than marketing executives give them credit for. In "One Digital Day," published in May 1998, and reprinted in part in the June 8, 1998, issue of *Fortune* magazine, 100 of the world's top photojournalists documented the worldwide impact of the microchip on modern life. The average consumer encounters no less than 70 microchips every day—in cars, cell phones, computers, microwave ovens, VCRs, thermostats, and just about everywhere you can imagine. Yet, marketers continue to debate the technology sophistication of the consumer.

Whether they are beepers carried by schoolchildren to receive messages from their parents, or at-home medical technology to test blood alcohol levels, or PCs to allow access to the Internet in the home or to do homework and keep track of taxes, consumer technology is here to stay. My older daughter sends digital pictures of my grandson from his day care center to my office in San Francisco and to his other set of grandparents in Paris over the Internet. My younger daughter successfully sold, via the Internet, arrangements of flowers that she grew herself. When the average person is that accepting of a virtual retail operation, it is clear that we have entered a very different world with few limits.

Nicolas at daycare and on my computer.

Technology gives consumers more options, and it changes buying habits. It is important that professionals understand the degree to which the world has already changed, although there's a sense that the real frontiers of the Knowledge Economy are still ahead. The emergence of the Internet as a vital link in the brand chain from producer to consumer means that brand strategists have to know how the Internet works and what it can do. There is no question that the Internet is growing. On-line ad revenues alone reached $2 billion in 1998, and by the year 2000 may be more than double that. That figure doesn't include the $20 billion invested in e-commerce, according to *New Media News*, a newsletter of the American Association of Advertising Agencies. Yahoo! has a headline that reads "Remember when people thought the Internet was a fad? Is 90 million people still considered a fad?" The number of consumers on-line has already surpassed that number, and broadband to the home—with its promise of ultrahigh-speed communication—is imminent. When that happens, the Internet will shortly become as ubiquitous as TV is today.

The rate of adoption of the Internet by consumers has been simply mind-boggling. Consider the following facts: It took 38 years for 50 million people to adopt radio; it took 16 years for 50 million people to adopt TV; and it took 4 years for 50 million people to adopt the Internet, once it became generally available.

Simple E-Mail to Complex E-Commerce—Just Do It

Talking about the Internet in a book is a very difficult task. Because of the speed of changes in this field, which is measured in days rather than years, whatever I say today is likely to be obsolete by the time you read it. Therefore, rather than attempting to give you the lowdown on the latest, I'd like to focus on convincing you that it is time to consider this powerful medium, if you are not yet convinced. I'd like to give you just a few broad concepts to think about in relation to branding and the World Wide Web: that a web brand is highly personal, that the Web fosters a brand community, and that the Web is the only truly global medium for the delivery of a brand message and a brand experience at the same time.

A typical new brand strategy that uses the Internet is Net.B@nk, which owns and operates the Atlanta Internet Bank. There are no tellers, no branches, none of the usual physical items that go into a traditional notion of a bank. Instead, the bank provides commercial and financial services, which can be accessed seven days a week, 24 hours a day from any personal computer. With over 7,000 customers and deposits of over $100 million, the bank is able to offer checking, money market accounts, and certificates of deposit, all with interest rates that reflect lower operating costs than traditional banks.

Born less than two years ago, the bank has used the Internet to establish its brand presence, not only as a way to link customers, but to define its essential difference with other competitors. The service isn't unique, but the delivery system over the Internet is. Of course, pioneers pay the price for venturing into the unknown, and home banking has been on the agendas of big banks for many years. How is a small start-up going to gain a toehold in this new medium? The people who run the Atlanta Internet Bank are very tech savvy. Their bankers use technology; the marketers use technology; and the salespeople use technology. They are part of the tech culture, and they are not afraid to use technology to help them brand their services. In essence, that's how brand professionals have to behave.

There are also banners and interstitial to consider in between the simplest and the most complex brand-building tools of the Internet. Everyone in the industry loves to say they hate banners. From the consumer's perspective, they are intrusive. From the ad agency's point of view, they are creatively limiting. From the marketer's vantage point, their effectiveness is difficult to measure. However, a recent study by the Internet Advertising Bureau and Millward Brown Interactive in San Francisco concluded that banner advertising significantly increased brand awareness and brand perception, in some cases as much as 300 percent. This study, and others like it, should help marketers think more openly about the Internet as a brand-building tool in addition to a transaction-making tool.

New Brands and Old–You Can Teach an Old Dog New Tricks

New corporate identities have been created in the last five years exclusively in the on-line world. Intuit, the financial software firm, noted mainly for its Quicken financial software and consumer tax preparation materials, is forging an on-line brand dedicated to providing consumer financial services. Want information about obtaining a mortgage? Forget driving to a bank. You can fire up your computer and read detailed descriptions of different types of mortgages, the status of your mortgage, and do just about everything associated with a mortgage, except stand in line.

Because the consumer is running the show, pointing and clicking throughout the experience, advertising plays a secondary role in the branding strategy. The brand lives as much through the look and feel of the site, and the experience of using it, as it does in the external communications about the service. Here are some questions to ask when evaluating the power of a business brand when operating in the virtual world:

- Is the brand experience consistent from the initial query to the final information?
- Is the site easy to use?
- Does it speak your language?
- How would you feel if, after a 30-minute tour of, perhaps, the wonderful world of mortgages, you were offered a toll-free 800 number rather than the ability to move directly to starting the mortgage approval process?
- Would you prefer to remain in a virtual environment rather than begin moving toward a person-to-person environment?

If the answers are yes, then it's clear the brand is operating effectively in the on-line world. The on-line brand experience requires the coordinated work of many more people than in the creation of a brand in the physical world. Not only are the advertising and marketing people involved, but also those who architect the on-line service itself, those who design the consumer interface, those who plan the actual elements of the service. Does this remind you of our earlier discussions about large numbers of decision makers in the new style of working?

Brands don't have to be brand new to use the Internet effectively. Consider wsj.com, the *Wall Street Journal's* interactive edition. As a fee-based service, it offers the readers the same information as the paper edition, but is distinctively formatted to fit the hectic schedules of people on-line. The advantage of timeliness, something that all electronic commerce can offer, is part of the intrinsic appeal of electronic information. In the case of wsj.com, however, the 165,000 subscribers are also able to access archived information, which the regular newsprint product cannot offer. They can also access price data and advertiser information. This enhanced service fits with the *Wall Street Journal's* brand promise to deliver the most comprehensive package of financial information and news.

The Toddler Years of TV and the Toddler Years of the Internet

There is a natural tendency when a new technology becomes available to try to replicate what we already know in that new technology. The first TV commercial looked remarkably like a radio spot—with a talking head reading a script. Then someone figured out, hey, we could change the scenery, make the actors move around, maybe even do a little skit. Some old-line ad agencies still refer to "copy strategy," a phrase that grew up in the early days of radio advertising, whether it is a TV ad or a radio or print execution. This is in contrast to agencies that started more recently, in which people talk about "creative platforms," allowing for the importance of visual imagery, music, editing style as much as for the "copy." In the early days of television, agencies and clients got involved in creating programming—making shows. The Texaco Star Theater was brought to you by Texaco. Then someone figured out, maybe we could make our own show and sell it to the advertiser willing to pay the most, or maybe split it up for a couple or more advertisers. Voila! Our modern model of the television industry—and, yes, radio is still alive and well.

Not surprisingly then, the very first applications of "advertising" on the Internet were web pages. The earliest versions, just three years ago, were essentially brochures reproduced electronically. Even the language "web page" is the language of print. The vast majority of web sites today are still essentially brochures, not unlike our talking-head radio commercials in the first years of TV. Today, everyone in the web world talks about creating content—the modern word for programming. However, just because that's what it is, doesn't mean that's what it will be. In three short years, we have already developed many more ideas about how to reach the consumer. The language of the Internet today includes words like banners, click-through rates, interstitials, portals, and the creation of community. The creative people working on the Internet deal not only with creative strategy, but also with site design, and architecture is now part of the lexicon. The days of "copy strategy" seem so simple by comparison.

We're Growing Up Fast

When I first started attending the National Association of Broadcasters Show in Las Vegas 5 years ago, where all the latest and the greatest in technology for the TV industry is exhibited, the show was all about hardware that was expected to last about 10 years. It was all analog, and it was all about getting TV and video production to be as good as film. For the first time the 1998 NAB felt to me more like the typical computer industry shows that I have been attending for years. The conversations were all about digital, about the transition of the industry to HDTV, about software, and about short life cycles. Even the exhibit style, the energy, and the urgency around the show were different that year. The 110,000 attendees from around the world found their way to the Sands Exhibition Center. This is the "secondary" exhibit hall where all the emerging companies, which don't have the ability yet to compete with the big guys, are bunched. There they were treated to advances in compression technologies, streaming video, and broadband distribution technologies—by terrestrial systems as well as satellite systems, all of which will allow commercials to be broadcast over the Internet. These commercials will be broadcast to tens of millions of personal computer users in the United States and around the world. The technology will allow for incredible degrees of customization, meaning we won't have to broadcast the same commercial to everyone. We'll even be able to change the commercials minutes before they air, adding local phone numbers, price updates, or other relevant local information.

These wonderful new technologies also contribute to a TV-like experience on a PC—with interaction. Now the technologies are available to overcome some of the creative limitations of the early days of the Internet. The graphics can be beautiful, rich, and powerful; music, motion, and drama can be integral. Special effects are possible, even more possible than with traditional film. Now, consumers can insert themselves as well with point and click. The consumer will decide how much of the content to allow and how much to interact. We, as marketers, have to learn a whole new way of thinking about broadcast that moves instantly with a click into conversation and a relationship.

Conditioned to the traditional phases of consumer awareness, consideration, trial, and purchase, we now have to deal with all these elements at one time. There is no orderly sequence anymore. Purchase behavior is as intuitive, fluid, concurrent, and random as our work styles. Perhaps the biggest change for both the consumer and the marketer will be that broadcasting a commercial on the Internet will not equate with delivering the mass audience in the same way it does with the TV. The consumer will be in the driver's seat with intelligent agents that will fan out over the Internet to get just those ads the consumer considers relevant. Now, the advertiser will be using other media to get people to watch Internet commercials.

Saturn, for example, has just launched a TV campaign designed to drive people to their web site. The clever commercials mimic pizza delivery with a salesperson dangling keys at the door with an "Anyone order a Saturn?" The Gap has a $20-million direct-mail campaign to boost sales at its on-line store. This is not a new phenomenon. America Online, Yahoo!, Excite, and Amazon.com, among others, have been using traditional media for several years. Gap and Saturn's campaigns, however, are indications of a sea change in attitude because they are not Internet companies, and because they are promoting a different distribution channel. Saturn's commercials send consumers to its web site instead of to a dealer. The Gap commercials direct consumers to go on-line instead of to their own storefront.

Today, more than 80 percent of all print ads already include a URL. This new model represents the confluence of powerful personal computers, the conversion of video from analog to digital and cost-effective terrestrial and satellite transmission of video-rich, or "fat," files. All this capability has helped shift brand power to the consumer in a big way. This is the kind of technology that is creating seismic shifts in the way branding, advertising, and marketing will operate.

Are You Convinced Yet?

If you are a manager who lets your lower-level people "play" on the Internet, you are wrong. If you think that only nerds build web pages, think again. You need to experience the same kind of chaos and confusion that consumers feel when they jump on the Internet and try to acquire information about products and services.

The advent of technology in such areas as travel and shipping is transforming these businesses and reducing costs for customers. FedEx, which started in the express letter business, is now reinventing itself to respond to the new reality of electronic document transfer. It will continue to be a viable company by helping to create just-in-time distribution for businesses and consumers by applying their routing and tracking systems to e-commerce. If you order by fax, phone, or on-line, FedEx will bring it to your door the next day. Services like Amazon.com would not be possible without a FedEx-type delivery system.

By the end of 1997, on-line purchasing was estimated at $5 billion. As the end of 1998 approached, it was said to be at $20 billion. This is not growth—it is an explosion. It isn't a gender thing, either. How often we hear from our clients that by a huge margin, the primary buyers of technology are males, between ages 25 and 49. This is not true. Women today account for 49 percent of on-line users, and America Online is telling us that 52 percent of their subscribers are women. Obviously, to be on-line, they have to be knowledgeable about computers, software, browsers, and search engines at the very least. The consumer has accepted technology as a fact of life. It's time that marketers did also.

The Facts of Brand Life on the Internet

One of the more interesting aspects of the Internet is that it embodies apparent contradictions. It is personal at the same time as it is about community. It is about relationships at the same time as it is global. These are powerful challenges that today's brand builder must confront.

Brand Is Personal

Technology, creatively used, can help a brand become even more personal. Whereas Internet sites are widely used for informational purposes, they can also generate powerful relationships to the brand. A wonderful example is Clinique, a cosmetics line owned by Estée Lauder Companies, which jumped into the on-line world, but did it in a way that respected its brand value. The company recognizes that part of the brand's unique appeal is linked as much to an in-store experience as to the hypoallergenic skin care products. Beauty advisers in white lab coats, scientific-looking counter displays, and personal attention are all ingredients that define the Clinique brand. In addition, Clinique has complex retail relationships with national and local department stores that could be jeopardized through on-line selling. As a result, Clinique can't put its line of cosmetics up for sale via the computer—the customer would not be getting the same brand experience in which the company has so heavily invested since it was launched in 1969. Instead, it operates an on-line registry, similar to a bridal registry, for people who would like to receive its products as gifts.

Clinique, however, has gone a step further by notifying potential gift givers about the registry. Clinique's electronic mail to gift givers includes an electronic link to its registry database and is managed in concert with retailer Macy's West.

Results to date have been encouraging. Designed as a seasonal program around the Christmas selling period, the sales goal was met five weeks into the first eight-week cycle. Average sales were also higher on-line, $58 versus $25 at the store counter. By using technology to link customers with the manufacturer and the retailer, Clinique was able to establish a greater bond between all three elements of the brand's retail experience. No one was left out. The brand established a personal relationship with the registrant, the gift giver, and the channel.

Yahoo!, the Internet's interactive card catalog, also reports early success. As a primary tool to help people navigate around the Internet, the company embarked on a strategy to define the Internet experience as fun and easy-to-use. In television commercials (such as "Do You Yahoo!?") the company compared normal life with life enhanced by using Yahoo!'s Internet search engine. Catch a small fish the regular way, catch a fish that looks like it's on steroids with Yahoo! The commercials were funny, off-the-wall, and upbeat— everything Yahoo! wants to be. There were no pictures of computers, no technical data flooding the screen. Yahoo! didn't even present itself as a technology company, but rather as a brand that promises outrageous results—something out of the ordinary. Using a variety of settings, Yahoo! promotes the richness of the Internet with tongue-in-cheek humor. Here is an example of a company willing to put traditional brand building ahead of tech speak.

Yahoo!'s alliance with publisher Ziff-Davis also emphasized the importance of the brand by creating a stand-alone magazine entitled *Yahoo! Internet Life,* which serves as a companion for the Internet experience. It would be as if Ford or GM teamed up with a publisher to produce *Road & Track* magazine. The Yahoo! brand became enmeshed in the life and daily routine of connecting to the Internet. In addition, the advent of the "My Yahoo! Online" feature engages the customer on a one-to-one basis, thereby establishing a relationship that continuously tracks and records the likes and dislikes of individuals. Making the experience personally satisfying says something about Yahoo!'s corporate mentality, rather than its technical know-how.

The brand can be made personal by the user experience as well. CDnow, unheard of two years ago, boasts being the world's largest music store, on-line. It is a 24-hour virtual store, which currently offers more than 250,000 titles. The company, started in 1994 by Jason and Matthew Olim in the basement of their parents' home, by the end of 1998 had over 200,000 customers. The company has recently embarked on a $10-million traditional ad campaign to burnish its brand image and promote on-line shopping. CDnow

"Do You Yahoo!?" TV frame.

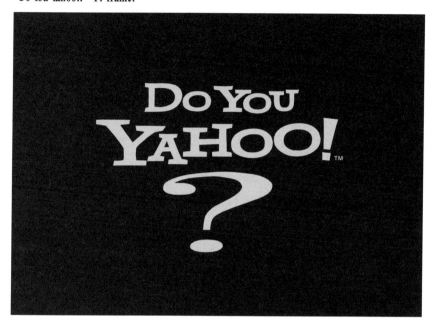

defines its brand as the set of experiences for those who buy from them. Want to listen to a sample of a recent release before you buy, click here. Want to check out reviews from other listeners? They are available, too. With no inventory, CDnow is building brand from the inside out, letting their customers define who they are and what they stand for.

The impetus for the company was Jason Olim's search for Miles Davis's records. With more than $6 million in sales in 1996 alone, Olim's vision of a place where customers could find a wide variety of music is becoming a reality. Using alliances with more than 9,000 fan-operated Internet sites, CDnow aims to connect directly with the people who are making the Internet community a viable commerce network. CDnow has more than 30 percent of the on-line market for music, and it makes those affiliations with other on-line sites a priority in its brand promise. Sites devoted to information for specific brands or specific types of music will now offer recordings from CDnow specifically chosen for that market.

Brand Is Community

Successful marketers must create just such on-line communities in which people can share ideas and information about products or services. Besides selling product, they are creating easily accessible forums in which conversation can take place about what people really want in their lives. The Internet is fertile ground for this. Tap into any Internet search engine to find out about a particular illness or disease and you will find groups of people—official and unofficial—who provide support, information, and experience.

Brand builders should not overlook the goodwill and emotional attachment people have toward these on-line communities. Reebok hosted a forum in which consumers asked questions about products, talked about their experiences with certain Reebok shoes, as well as recent sporting events. The on-line experience wasn't about selling shoes; it was about the lives of the people communicating. It gave the participants the chance to become a living part of the Reebok brand. And, more important, it gave Reebok a more integrated brand campaign. Collaboration with the consumer pumped life into the brand.

Brand Is Global

Following the crash of SwissAir Flight 111, from JFK to Geneva in August, 1998, the *San Francisco Chronicle* called me for an opinion on the use of the Internet to communicate information about the crash. My reaction was, surprisingly, that the Internet might be better suited to help everyone cope with the crisis than traditional news channels. When a tragedy like this happens, those who are the closest to it are starved for information, any tidbit, that can help them cope with the reality that is so hard to face. Communicating with everyone on a real-time basis is nearly impossible when information is just being uncovered by the minute, much less even finding everyone who is touched by the tragedy. Even before the airline was able to release a passenger manifest, it was clear that this event would touch families around the globe in a very personal way. There is no vehicle that has the ability to be global, personal, and instantaneous at the same time other than the Internet. My response was, that as long as the site was extremely sensitive to the feelings of the victim's families, this was an excellent response to a very difficult situation, and SwissAir should be commended for recognizing the needs of the families—and the flying public—for information.

The power of the Internet as a global force extends beyond product and service marketing, and it affects politics and the marketing of politicians. The fact that Congress chose to release the *Starr Report* on the Clinton-Lewinsky affair on the Internet made it instantaneously a global political event with far-reaching consequences.

Whenever anything is posted on the Web, it belongs immediately to the world. There are no boundaries, no borders, no syndication rights, and attempts at censorship have been largely unsuccessful. That's part of the power and part of the complexity of the Internet. Every brand is instantly a global brand, whether it was intended or unintended. As marketers, much more attention needs to be paid to this simple fact. We can no longer be as comfortable in our U.S. centricity if we are to take advantage of this wonderful tool for global marketing. Once again, the concept behind the brand becomes important, and the concept must connect with core human issues that transcend fads and narrow cultural idioms.

A Tool for Building Relationships

Jumping into the on-line electronic commerce sea is not an invitation to change and modify your brand strategy. It becomes a tool to articulate and sculpt the brand in a modern, vital context. Combining the opportunities of electronic commerce with the advantages of now very low-cost data storage (it is 1,000 times cheaper to keep a customer name and address on a computer than it was 20 years ago) should give retailers—and manufacturers—a clearer picture of what is happening in the marketplace. If they seize the opportunities that this easily sortable information gives them, innovators will find that this technology becomes a bridge to build real-time dialog with customers. Technology will facilitate conversations and service, giving companies a chance to maintain binding relationships.

9

The Brand Audit as a Tool for a Fast-Moving World

Brand audits, or assessments, are nothing new. They've been a staple of the marketing and advertising worlds for as long as brands have existed. Just about every marketer, agency, marketing consultant, and research group has conducted audits of brand personalities, attributes, strengths, and weaknesses. There are about as many flavors of brand auditing, both qualitative and quantitative, as there are agencies and consultancies that do it.

Fundamentally, almost all brand assessments or audits incorporate conversations with consumers on the phone, in one-on-one interviews or focus groups, or use diary panels. Some have added analogies, role playing, and just about every other imaginable technique to draw out insights about what makes up the brand. They probe around the importance of various product performance issues and cost/value trade-offs. They explore where and how brands fit into the lives of their users. They pretty much all have various models and visual tools, such as perceptual maps,

competitive matrices, value hierarchies, and others, to try to capture and encapsulate all of the information that was gathered.
Why am I talking about old news now?

What's New?

Short Life Cycle Products–Massive Change–Uncertain Future

Let me dust off the concept of *brand audit*, or *brand assessment* as I
prefer to call it, and put in a few new wrinkles that, in my experience, have dramatically improved the success rate of warp-speed
branding. The world of technology has required us to significantly
modify our approach to brand audits. First, we are often dealing
with products of technology innovation, so that there is no brand,
per se, to audit yet. That's just one of the reasons that I prefer the
terminology of *brand assessment*. Second, we are talking about very
short life cycle products, massive change, and uncertain futures.
Third, we are always dealing with some degree of complexity in
the Brand Ecosystem.

As I began to realize how different our clients were in these
areas, I called my good friend and trusted consultant, Steven
Cristol, who now works out of Seattle, to come help us think
through how to approach some of these issues. With Steven's help,
my colleagues and I came to understand that traditional brand
audit methodologies used by packaged-goods and large service
company brands, no matter what research technique is being used,
typically focus on defining the brands as they exist *today*. Such
assessments are based on current experiences, behaviors, and perceptions, all of which makes sense when brands change slowly
over time and a current snapshot is a satisfactory start. When a
brand already exists, it's also possible to put primary emphasis on
exploring how the brand is perceived by its actual consumers,
because they are traditionally the only significant stakeholders.

This reflects the simple structure of one brand, one brand audience, which was the norm.

Assessing technology brands, we have found, requires a more complex approach—an approach that takes into account the fundamental nature of technology markets and the impact of technology innovations on the entire marketing system. Just as the techniques of brand building that have emerged from technology companies require new ways of working, the process of learning about brands also needs to be reengineered to reflect the unique characteristics of technology markets. Here's where we ended up, a process we have used numerous times with great success.

At first glance, the Brand Assessment Methodology Chart may look similar to audits and assessments that you have seen or even used before. However, if you'll examine it more closely, you'll see that *there are subtle but substantive* differences. The main difference is that it requires the user not only to take a snapshot of the brand as it is today, but to chart how the brand is likely to develop tomorrow or over the near term. In addition, it demands an organic approach, because in high tech we've found brands don't exist in a static environment in the marketplace. This dynamic/organic approach to branding, drawn from the high-tech world, but applicable to many other industries, provides brand stewards a much deeper understanding of their brand and helps chart brand growth in a much more effective manner.

Collect the Information in Person

We've all heard the phrase "garbage in, garbage out." If the information you collect is not good enough, or as I prefer to say, "rich enough," it will be much harder to draw meaningful conclusions. Now, obviously, there are many skilled researchers and interviewers who can in fact collect very solid information. The difficulty lies in the fact that it is not information we are after, but insight.

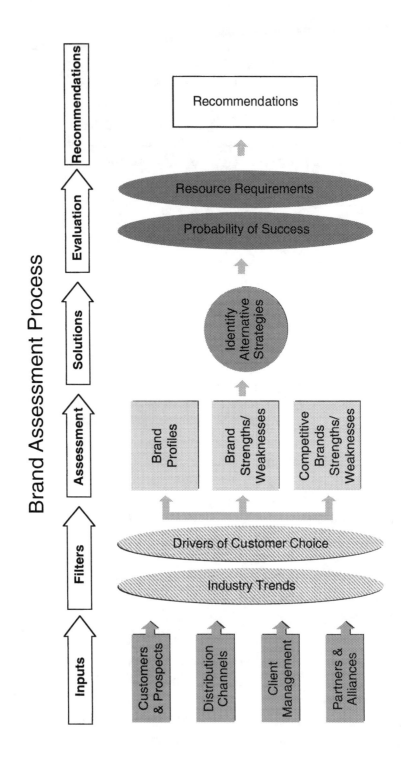

Often, it is insight about a product, or even a whole new category of products, that is new to the person with whom we are talking, so they are not necessarily very articulate about the subject.

The process we have developed requires first a rough outline of areas to probe. We then video- or audiotape all the interviews or observations so that we can keep referring to consumer feelings when we begin to develop the strategy matrices. Another important piece of the methodology that we developed, out of convenience originally, was that, rather than hire outside facilitators or interviewers, we used our own people to conduct all interviews— *the very same people who will then be involved in crafting the strategy.* This ensures that our people begin to develop brand insights and a gut instinct for the brand—not by listening to someone else's interview on a tape or through a one-way mirror, but by looking right into the consumer's eyes and trying to get out of the consumer real feelings about the brand that will help us in the brand development process.

We really learned the importance of this in early 1998 when we conducted a brand assessment for CyberStar, a brand new company delivering satellite-based broadband communications services. No consumers were able to tell us what that could be and business buyers immediately focused on land-based solutions and dismissed the possibility of reliable and effective satellite-based approaches. Because there was no other company delivering the same service, there were no competitors to talk about or relate to. Naturally, what to ask to get the appropriate insights becomes more of an issue when talking about new ideas, new concepts, and new ways of doing things.

Because CyberStar had so many constituents in its Brand Ecosystem—consumers in both the home and business, partners, strategic allies, applications developers, and more—and because all of these people were scattered around the globe and the client was in a big hurry, we deviated from our usual approach of having our own people conduct all our conversations and hired a very reputable research firm to do some of the interviews. We quickly realized we had made a major mistake.

When dealing with totally new areas, it is simply not possible to outline in advance what needs to be found out. The process needs to be much more organic. If the researcher does not have a personal stake in developing the strategy and is not familiar with the methodology we designed to get at brand strategy in an innovative environment, the information collected is often simply not what leads to good insights. We found that our research firm, in its desire to stick with the assignment, kept to the discussion outline at the expense of mining the veins that the respondents uncovered for us, which is often where much of the rich insight is found.

This is a subtle but very powerful point. The researcher cannot really know when to take liberties if the research is not linked tightly to strategy. This theme of integration of disciplines and close collaboration should already be familiar to you, either through your own experience or from discussion in the earlier chapters. Needless to say, we had to redo a number of the interviews for CyberStar at our own expense.

Gathering information for insight will not always be in the form of interviews. When we were working on the introduction of the first Sony PC, we actually sent our planners into people's homes to *observe* what they did with computers to help us gain insights for our brand. Sometimes we devise games to play. For RenoAir, we drew a series of pictures of the process of buying tickets, going to the airport, and actually boarding the airplane and asked consumers to fill in the dialog in the conversation balloons.

The bottom line, as I learned over the years, is that information gathering and brand strategy development need to be very closely linked. It's best when the strategists are gathering the information themselves.

The inputs (the first column of the methodology diagram) come from many more sources than just customers. The one-on-ones we conduct involve as much of the Brand Ecosystem as is pos-

RenoAir account planning.

Brand assessment inputs—go out and talk to stakeholders.

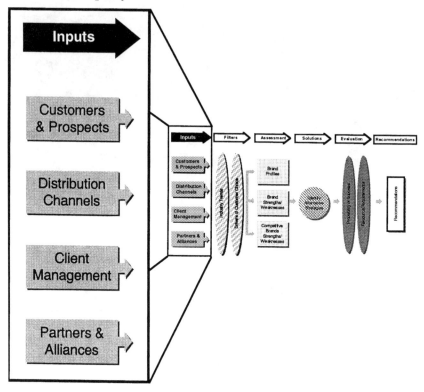

sible to touch. Today's technology brands exist in a fluid, con-stantly changing state, with multiple constituencies and a far broader audience of stakeholders. The consumer may still hold center stage, but brand development must address an extended audience, including such groups as sales and distribution, alliance and joint venture partners, management and employees, and industry and financial analysts. For CyberStar, we also had to talk with market and financial analysts, because their biases would directly affect the trade press who would then write about the cat-egory in magazine articles, which would be read and affect, in turn, the customers. Back to our Brand Ecosystem.

The filters we put on the information refer to how we select out the data points and insights that we need to eventually craft the

Brand assessment filters–look for trends that predict the future.

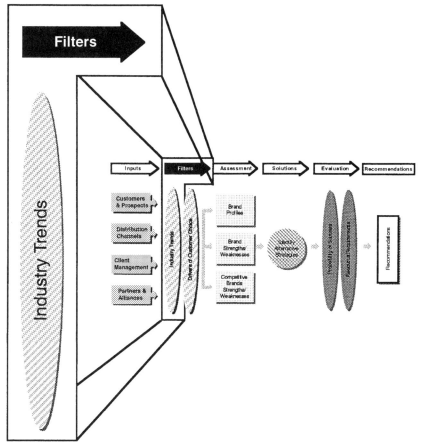

strategy. The first filter we use is the filter of *industry trends*. Technology markets change with incredible speed, so a snapshot of a
brand today may have far less value than an assessment that com-
bines today's reality with tomorrow's expectations. This makes it
essential to examine emerging market, consumer, and even social
trends that will impact the future strength of the brand, so the
brand promise can be crafted to address today's reality as well as
the unpredictable future. These trends may not always be obvious,
because the inherent nature of technology markets is that there is

a domino-like effect in which seemingly unrelated developments can have a powerful influence on the brand. For example, in 1995, we conducted an extensive brand audit in the television broadcasting industry for Tektronix, headquartered in Beaverton, Oregon (which, along with Sony, is one of the leading companies in the field). We found several emerging trends that foreshadowed the whole gut-wrenching change in the industry to digital television, which the industry is now undergoing.

We found that this hardware-oriented, capital-intensive industry in which typical expenditures were expected to last 8 to 11 years, was beginning to realize that the future lay less in hardware and more in software. Even before the manufacturers, the customers began to realize that their world needed to move from analog to digital. New and younger management and staff were entering the field, and these people were much more computer literate. Having grown up in the age of the PC, they were aware of and comfortable with the capabilities of the PC and wanted to drag these capabilities into the professional broadcast equipment. If they could get special effects easily on their home PCs, why couldn't they on their professional consoles? If they could edit and add graphics in real time when they were working on their hobbies, why did they have to wait for video to be shipped in from the field? They wanted to be able to receive images in real time while news was breaking, edit it on the fly, and beat all the other stations to air.

Along with this comfort with the digital world, we also uncovered an emerging trend toward joint decision making about new equipment, including news, engineering, and creative departments and involving both management and staff. This was replacing the engineering-centered decision making of the past. (This sounds a lot like elements of the new way of working I talked about earlier.) This emerging new workforce was familiar with networked computing, so they understood issues of open architectures and standards, and the critical importance of software as the television broadcasting industry began to move toward the digital future. Today, less than a handful of years later, TV broadcast brands that rely only on the traditional audience, and on traditional values based on engineering excellence, are doomed to a shaky future. With our trend identification methodology, however, we were able to help Tektronix craft a brand strategy that could help it transition from where the industry was at the time to the new reality.

The second filter we use is what we call *drivers of choice*. Here, we sift through all the information to collect insights on how each stakeholder group goes about evaluating and/or making intuitive decisions that may affect our brand choice.

Brand assessment filters–drivers of choice to identify what makes the customer choose one brand over another.

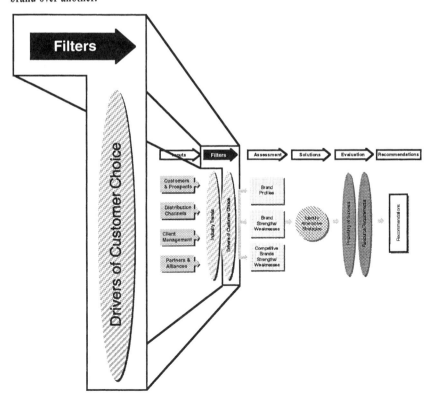

A number of years ago we were working for FMC, one of the top manufacturers of U.S. farm equipment. They make million-dollar tomato harvesters and fruit-picking equipment, among other things, which they sell to farmers all over the world. The client had spent a considerable amount of money on research and had provided us with a research-based marketing brief that concluded that *reliability* was the determining factor in brand choice. Their directive to us was to focus on all the features of the equipment that supported product reliability.

Well, we wanted to put some life and some emotion into the brief to get more effective advertising, so we went out into the field—literally. We spoke to the farmers out on their tractors, in their four-wheel vehicles, and at their kitchen tables. We found out that for the most part, these were family businesses, and everyone, including the wife and the children, was often involved. Life for them was very uncertain. They were at the mercy of Mother Nature for their crops. They were often somewhat undercapitalized, so that if they had a poor harvest their family income would suffer directly. The farm was not an investment for them—it was their family's livelihood.

When we got to the issue of reliability, over and over they told us that FMC products never broke down. Why, then, did the earlier research point to reliability as the major driver of choice? This was particularly puzzling, as FMC business had declined significantly, yet their products were the strongest in the industry in terms of all product features and characteristics, and they were recognized as such by the farmers. Well, it was one of those conversations with the husband and wife, sitting at their kitchen table sharing a cup of coffee, that led to the insight. What the written questionnaire had pointed to was *reliability*—that was the box the respondents had checked. When the conversation became friend to friend rather than researcher to respondent, what the farmer and his wife actually meant was that FMC had been in the business before with pea pickers, and they abandoned that business in some kind of reorganization. Therefore, if you had a pea picker from FMC, there was no one to call about parts, refurbishing, new features, or sometimes just emotional support. All of the farmers had talked about that with each other and were very aware. They knew that FMC had "abandoned" them.

We found out that *reliability* had nothing to do with *product* reliability. The farmers needed to know that the supplier of their expensive machinery would stick with them through good years and bad years and not leave them high and dry. The farmers had really meant *company* reliability, but the research techniques had been unable to differentiate that powerful and important difference. The campaign that came out of this insight was photography of farmers and their families living their daily lives in a very *National Geographic* style—no product-as-hero shots. The tag line was "We also grew up on the family farm."

We knew we had struck a nerve here when the posters that we printed for dealers, based on the print advertising, became the single, most requested pieces of collateral by the farmers. They wanted to take them home and hang them in their offices, kitchens, and barns. FMC had shown them that they understood the life of the farmer and that they could empathize. Here was an emotion-based strategy for a million-dollar piece of equipment, and it produced $75 million in sales in the first year of the campaign. Hopefully, you'll now appreciate the importance of really understanding the drivers of choice and how much difference real insight can make in crafting brand strategies.

The next stage is the *assessment stage*. Here, we try to depict brands in all dimensions as much as possible. We try to understand what the brand would look like, feel like, smell like, and even sound like—if it could speak or emit a smell. People often have trouble explaining the emotional qualities they attach to a brand. If you ask someone what they think of Lucent Technologies—it's just a couple of words or the result of an ad they saw. However, when you begin to ask them what a technology company called

192

FMC campaign.

"Sure I could buy a new car. But that won't make me money."

What do you do with someone who invests a fortune in a hunk of iron, but won't spend a few thousand on a new car?

Someone who makes more than a few sacrifices to his life's work. His farm.

One thing you better do is provide a piece of farm machinery that's going to work as hard as he does. That's going to recover more product than any other machine. That's going to make him money.

For over four generations, one company has done just that.

And we'll keep on doing it.

Food Processing Machinery Division, 2300 Industrial Avenue, Madera, California 93639, (209) 661-3200.

 **FMC**

We also grew up on the family farm.

193

Lucent, spun off from AT&T, might cook if it were a chef at a great restaurant, you suddenly get all kinds of strange answers, which begin to reveal the associations the consumer has with a name or a brand. We often find that these descriptors are richer in terms of understanding a brand than words.

For example, when we asked management what Loral, a major U.S. space and satellite communications company would sound like, we got a response that it would be jazz. Why? Because it was made up of all kinds of disparate companies, strategies, and styles, but somehow it all worked together. When we asked the broadcast industry to characterize the major brands, the pictures they put together told the following story:

Brand assessment–brand profiles.

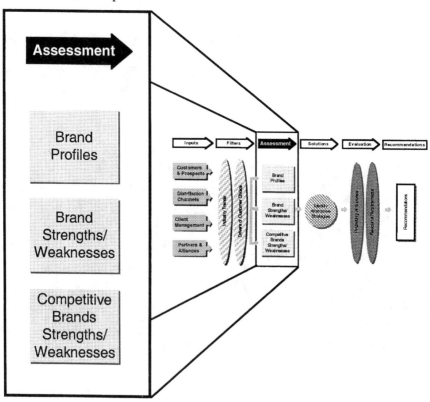

Brand A was an earnest, dedicated, knowledgeable engineer who was slightly awkward. He had a mustache and wore a plaid shirt with a pocket protector. He was characterized as helpful, a good Samaritan who was on the customer's side. Brand B, on the other hand, was characterized as an easy-going hippie wearing a baseball cap who "really understands my business." He is a little geeky. He is also complacent, a little behind the times, no longer as dependable today. As a matter of fact, he is like the high school sweetheart you wouldn't want to marry today. This last statement gave us a wealth of insight in crafting a brand. We noticed, going through all the transcripts and videos, that while Brand B was always uppermost in the customers' minds and generally favorable comments were made, it was the only brand that was always, without exception, referred to in the past tense. It was an important insight for our whole strategy group think—more about that in a moment.

Brand C was viewed as a polished, rich, powerful, and extremely capable man. He was always well dressed in a very nice suit. He was also a good negotiator, a bad listener, and had an agenda. Brand D, on the other hand, was a hip Mac-head with a ponytail. He gave off the aura of a used-car salesman with pointy shoes, too much aftershave, and lots of chains, but "I have to deal with him" because he has what I want.

What these characterizations should tell you is the subtle, emotional qualities that drive brands and exist below the surface in the minds of consumers. This process can work for existing brands like Maxwell House Coffee, which has a brand history extending over 100 years—or for a brand that is totally new, for which the territory is wide open, and discussions will turn toward want and respect more than actual experience with the brand.

When it's time to actually begin crafting the brand strategy, we have found it most useful to approach that process in a group setting rather than anoint any one person as the strategy guru. We typically schedule two or three sessions of several hours to begin populating the various matrices that we need to craft a strategy.

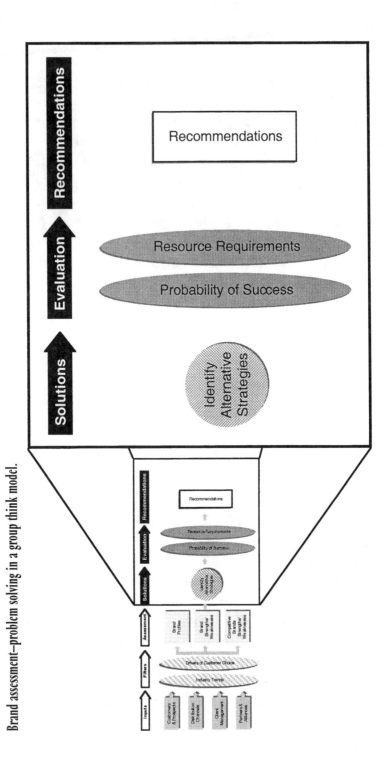

Brand assessment—problem solving in a group think model.

Everyone who conducted interviews and observations comes into one room with multiple electronic whiteboards. This helps us capture the thoughts of the group and be ready to get them into presentation form almost immediately with just some minor editing. We've already talked about identifying trends. Typically, we just list them out as everyone consults their individual notes. We then have a lively discussion about the rank ordering and prioritizing of the trends for our brand.

The next thing we try to capture is the drivers of choice by each of the appropriate market segments. Again, we prioritize for each segment and then begin to look for common threads. This is very important, because even though our marketing messages may be tailored to individual segments, our brand strategy must be able to encompass all the constituencies, must be timeless, and must be deliverable. Following is a snapshot of part of the drivers-of-choice matrix for the broadcast/video industry prepared in 1996.

Drivers of choice, we have found, have at least two dimensions even for very expensive business-to-business purchases—both rational and emotional. Our brand assessment process attempts to

Brand assessment—drivers of choice—for the broadcast industry.

Broadcast	Production/Post	Corporate/ Industrial	Telcos	Vertical Applications
Reliability	Artistic feature set (software)	Cost	Service/support	Architecture
Picture quality	Client demand for brand	Service/support	Reliability	Innovation
Service/support	Service/support	Assistance with business case for capital	Picture quality	Reliability
Integration	Reliability	Ease of use	Open systems	Cost savings
Cost savings	Image (of vendor brand)	Reliability	Server expertise	Service/support
Delivers on commitments	Open systems	Picture quality	Price/value	Open systems

Common drivers across all markets: ● Reliability   ▪ Service/support   ▫ Software driven capture both. This is a critical element of good branding and good communications of all forms, and especially advertising, which is the most powerful way to tap into the emotional drivers.

Next, we work up the brand profiles. Our planners work on making a visual depiction either with a short film or with mood boards—collages of photos that in sum total depict what we found out. Finally, when these exercises are finished, our group of strategists is able to hash out several alternative brand strategies that take all we have learned into account. The final steps involve an analysis of the feasibility of the winning strategies and a recommended strategy with possibly one alternative. Some of our clients get involved at just these last stages, whereas some of our clients like to be briefed on our findings as we go along and participate in

Drivers of choice–rational and emotional example from the broadcast industry.

DRIVER	RATIONAL	EMOTIONAL
Reliability	■ Uptime ■ Does what it's supposed to	■ Trustworthiness ■ Comfort
Service/support	■ Responsiveness ■ Delivers on commitments ■ Customization ■ Customer involvement in product strategy	■ Human relationships ■ Accessibility ■ Really understands my business
Software expertise	■ Integration —With what customer has —Systems solutions with third parties ■ Networking ■ Openness	■ Innovative ■ Cool ■ Enables creative possibilities

some of the group thinking. In general, we have found that col-laboration tends to work a little better for two reasons. First, when the client participates in the process, the client gets a deeper understanding of the findings, right along with us. Second, because there are no surprises, there is better buy-in. Our client has to be bought in to be able to sell through his or her organization and to be able to develop the internal communications programs required to get the organization behind the brand strategy.

Sounds Like a Lot of Work—How Does It Help Warp-Speed Branding?

Our brand assessment process is the result of successes and failures over the years. We are now very pleased with how it works. The process is fluid enough to accommodate the specific needs of each situation, and yet there is a discipline behind it. It's still flexible enough to adapt to different brand- or industry-specific situations. We consider it vital to warp-speed branding. It may take a little extra effort in the conceptual and analytical phase—but it adds a clarity that is essential when you begin to disseminate the brand strategy to all the constituents of the Brand Ecosystem.

Having a strategy in place—an architecture, in a sense—helps keep everyone on the same page. At the same time, it becomes the fabric on which every other brand action or decision can be assessed. Decisions about whether we should go this way or that become much easier and substantially faster when there is a brand strategy in place against which the decision can be assessed. Tactical programs can be developed much more quickly when there is a brand framework to work in. Each decision can be measured against whether this will support the brand, be neutral, or take away from the brand. I like to think of brand decisions in terms of an equity account in the brand bank. Then, when it's time to make a decision, I evaluate whether this will add to the brand equity, subtract from it, or have no impact. I try to steer clients to decisions that will add to the brand equity. If it were a neutral event, I'd like them to think if there is a way to reshape it to make it add to the brand equity account. If it will take away from the brand equity bank, then I want them to consider if it is worth it and if this action will eventually pay off.

When you decide that it's time to speed up your own branding processes, either as an offensive or defensive move, I hope you can implement some of the learnings I've shared with you here, which represent about 20 years' experience in fast-moving markets.

10

How Ready Are You for Warp-Speed Branding?

Everyone loves a quiz. Here's a little one to help you determine your readiness for warp-speed branding. Good luck.

Warp-Speed Branding Quiz

SECTION 1

	YES	NO
1. Does everyone have access to the Web?	☐	☐
2. Is remote access available to those who are likely to use it?	☐	☐
3. Is there a defined telecommuting policy?	☐	☐
4. Does your company tend to rely on voice mail over e-mail?	☐	☐

---

5. Does your organization have experience in collaborating with other companies for critical projects? ☐ ☐

6. Is time to market a concept that's known throughout your company? ☐ ☐

Points: 1 point for each "Yes."
Multiply your score by 3 and fill in total.

☐ Total

SECTION 2

	Yes	No
7. Is telecommuting done informally?	☐	☐
8. Are cross-functional teams common?	☐	☐
9. Do you have walled offices?	☐	☐
10. Do you have meetings more frequently than you write and distribute memos?	☐	☐
11. Is there a structure around how new ideas are brought to management's attention?	☐	☐
12. Are ideas generated informally and budgeted as they are approved?	☐	☐
13. Does your organization make decisions quickly?	☐	☐

	A Lot	Modest	Little
14. Is there a lot of interaction between departments, a modest amount, or little to none?	☐	☐	☐
15. Is there a lot of interaction between divisions, a modest amount, or little to none?	☐	☐	☐

Points: 1 point for each "Yes."
Multiply your score by 2 and fill in subtotal.

☐

Give yourself 2 points for "A Lot" and 1 point for "Modest" and fill in subtotal.

☐

Add subtotals:

☐ Total

SECTION 3

	YES	NO
16. Do you have a central repository for intellectual property?	☐	☐
17. Is e-commerce part of your plan?	☐	☐
18. Does your company have an overall brand manager?	☐	☐

Points: 1 point for each "Yes."
Multiply your score by 2 and fill in total.

Total

SECTION 4

	YES	NO
19. Is there a company initiative around knowledge management?	☐	☐
20. Does the CIO report to the CEO?	☐	☐

Points: 1 point for each "Yes."
Fill in total.

Total

SECTION 5

	YES	NO
21. Do you have all customer information centralized in one place?	☐	☐
22. If you sell through channels, do you have any mechanism for identifying the end user?	☐	☐

Points: 1 point for each "Yes."
Multiply your score by 2 and fill in total.

Total

Section 6

	Yes	No
23. Is your customer service and support organization integrated with the sales organization?	☐	☐
24. Does marketing have access to customer information?	☐	☐
25. Do you have a web site?	☐	☐
26. Do your agencies talk to each other regularly?	☐	☐
27. Have your agencies ever met in one room to discuss your business?	☐	☐
28. Do you have a budget for on-line advertising?	☐	☐

Points: 1 point for each "Yes."
Fill in total.

┌─────┐
└─────┘
Total

Section 7

	Yes	No
29. Is your company IT investment above 3 percent of sales?	☐	☐
30. Do your IT investments tend to be about gaining productivity?	☐	☐
31. Do your IT investments tend to be about new capability? (*Give yourself 2 points for a "Yes"*).	☐	☐

Points: 1 point for each "Yes" except as marked
and fill in total.

┌─────┐
└─────┘
Total

┌─────┐
└─────┘
Grand Total

And Now for the Scoring

Add up your "Yes" answers, multiply them by the points indicated, and place your score for each section in the right-hand box. Add up the total of the right-hand boxes for your grand score.

If you got 58 points or more, you are already operating at warp speed. You should be writing this book. Anything over 45 points means you have a healthy appreciation of what it takes to move quickly. If you scored below 25, you should consider selling your company while you still can.

How to Improve Your Readiness

If you asked me today which is the most important, I'd answer, based on my observation of hundreds of companies who have succeeded and many who have not, that culture is probably the single most important issue to focus on for warp-speed branding to be successful. If the right culture is there, one that is decisive, communicative, and collaborative, it is not so difficult to bring in the infrastructure and the marketing expertise. If the culture is not amenable to some of the principles we have been discussing over the past few chapters, then the changes required to get you to warp-speed branding will be gut wrenching.

That doesn't mean that you should abandon any thoughts of moving to this brave new world. Just understand that it will be difficult at best. Culture is the hardest thing to change in a company, because it cannot be legislated. It requires strong leadership, strong commitment, and perseverance. The rewards, however, are many. They include the ability to get to market faster, a better integrated brand that bonds with the infrastructure and provides all the rewards of a relationship versus a transaction. In addition, the work style required to make it happen unleashes more of the potential of the knowledge workers you have on your own staff.

My own agency has been through two or three stages of evolution in culture, each bringing it closer to the new reality and each very difficult transitions for the agency as an institution and for the people. Over the years, the changes involved moving into open-plan office space, which we did around 1984 when the concept was still very new. It involved moving to networked computers and file sharing in the mid-1980s. Then we moved into the really difficult areas of getting people to share work and half-baked thoughts with each other, to collaborate on ideas, and to think of themselves as a team. Building the technology infrastructure to support this kind of work was actually the easy part—getting people coming from all different kinds of agencies to work differently was more of a challenge. The pain, however, was worth it in the end, as it has helped us break new ground with our clients.

Epilogue

In late October of 1998, I had the good fortune to attend the annual meeting of the Committee of 200, a powerful organization of women business owners and high-level corporate managers, representing many different industries from financial services to retailing, from manufacturing to oil exploration.

As I sat and listened to the panelists in a presentation called "Energy in Your Future," I was struck by the realization that there seemed to be no industry left untouched by the drive for innovation, for greater customer choice, and for speed to market to gain a competitive advantage—all of the factors that make warp-speed branding a necessity. There is no better example of the gut-wrenching changes that embody most of the principles of warp-speed branding than the deregulation of the utilities industry in the United States. I learned that as of October 1998, 18 states, representing 48 percent of the U.S. population, had passed laws deregulating the gas and electrical utilities within their states.

From a consumer's point of view, it was a drive to create options by providing more choices and reduced prices. From the utility's point of view, it would create new business opportunities and a need for whole new skill sets in operating in a competitive environment. For the industry as a whole, it would be a complete restructuring in how the industry operates that would raise some fundamental strategic questions. Who provides what piece of the service? What *is* the service? How is money made in the new environment?

In California, the first state to implement this deregulation, the initial push came from energy-dependent businesses that were threatening to leave California because of its exceptionally high rates for gas and electricity as set by the Public Utilities Commission. Consumer interests, however, lay more in choice: some wanted lower rates; others preferred one service and one bill for telecommunications, cable, and utilities services; still others were interested in green energy and were willing to pay more for service that is environmentally friendly.

For the industry itself, deregulation means a major reformation from a vertically integrated industry in which generation, transmission, distribution, and customer service (including hookup, meter reading, billing, and so forth) were all handled by one company. Today in California, and the many states to follow, deregulation will create a whole new Brand Ecosystem. It will be a significant redefinition of *what* service the brands who will play are to provide. It will also mean a drive to shorten time to market for new services and new products to win market share, to own the customer relationship, and ultimately to create value for the shareholders of the companies investing in this new world.

Pacific Gas and Electric (PG&E), our venerable supplier in northern California, will have to battle Shell Oil, among others, who will be vying for its customers. After much consumer study, Shell has determined that the strength of its brand, over 12 million credit card customers, and the largest retail gas operation in North America, will permit it to go directly to consumers in their homes and provide them with their power. When measured on innovation, longevity, and service levels, consumers in California rated the Shell brand equal with PG&E, opening a whole new business for Shell and providing PG&E with an instant and formidable competitor.

They aren't the only ones who will be entering the fray. Cable operators, telcos, credit card companies, and even insurance companies are all eyeing the possibilities of extending their brands into this arena, all vying for the enviable position as *the* brand of the wired home.

An industry that was, up until now, a pretty simple industry, with only fuel suppliers and a network of regional utility companies, will now blossom into some kind of complex multibrand structure, which at this point we cannot even define. Already in California, the simple supplier/seller model has been broken up into a complex system, which now includes a power exchange that operates like a stock market for power and oversees bidding and selling of various types of power in real time. It includes an Independent Service Operator organization to oversee the reliability of energy transmission for the consumer, and it includes many energy service providers who will actually service the customer. The Brand Ecosystem will begin to include not only the Shells, the telcos, and the cable companies, but all kinds of new companies that will be formed either from the ground up or as partnerships, alliances, or mergers of known brand names with a franchise for reliability in the home. It will be the Wild West frontier all over again—and all other states will be watching to see how things progress as they develop their own approaches.

Here is a staid, organized, established industry being thrown into technological change, the need for rapid innovation, and speed of decision and implementation, and as a result, the need to build a whole new brand relationship with the consumer.

All of this coming industry chaos and customer confusion are actually normal by-products of change and innovation, and it is in this kind of environment that the brand becomes ever more important. The brand, in its unique relationship with the consumer, becomes the shortcut to "trust" when there is too much choice and difficulty in assessing alternatives. Notice, I did not say *lack of information*, because there is plenty of information. *Assessing* the information, boiling it down to something manageable, and making a decision with some sense of security is ultimately the responsibility of the informed consumer. The brand relationship is a significant piece of the assessment process. In a climate of chaos and ambiguity, it is the brand that endures and the brand that creates the climate for financial success for the company that is innovating.

In the World of Brand, Creative Is King

In the last several chapters I have given you many examples of how the brand world has changed. There is, however, a significant point of continuity from the enduring brands of the past and our complex brand organisms of today. With complicated Brand Ecosystems, more consumer involvement than ever, and a proliferation of media, it is the creative expression of the brand that creates the powerful imprint on the consumer's mind and cuts through the clutter.

We all know about media overload. There's too much television, too much print; there's radio and the Internet. Even gas pumps now double as electronic billboards, telling us to drink Pepsi while we pump our gas. In this kind of media glut, it is the outstanding pieces of creative that make a mark and become bits of popular culture: TV commercials like "Got Milk?" from Goodby Silverstein and Partners, and print like Apple's "Think Different" campaign.

In the 1960s, 1970s, and 1980s, sound, moving images, emotion, and reach—all served to make television, and in particular network television, the vehicle of choice. Its expense in production and cost of media was mitigated by the lack of anything else that even approached its appeal. Today, however, network executives are all lamenting declining viewership and the erosion of viewers to cable networks and now increasingly to competing activities like surfing the Net.

Up until recently, the Web was too primitive a medium to create powerful images and evoke strong emotions. Beginning, however, with Macromedia's Shockwave, technology for lifelike animation and full-motion video on the Internet is becoming more sophisticated and reliable. Real Networks' Real Audio and Real Video products currently on the market make the Internet home to radio broadcasts and archival video clips, all on an individual basis. The new mix of media will demand more and more customized creative work to appeal to specific target audiences, and it will be accessed increasingly through their computers.

At the 1998 National Association of Broadcasters convention in Las Vegas, companies were able to demonstrate satellite systems that could broadcast customized advertisements directly to a desktop PC. It will be a while before every advertiser adapts to the new possibilities, but it is time for the leaders to innovate now. Each successive technology revolution has been adopted faster than conventional wisdom believed. It's time to learn how to develop creative that works in traditional media as well as the new. They won't be new for long.

Even in the world of television, new technology offers tantalizing opportunities for displaying creative. Ads can be placed literally on the screen when and where the broadcaster feels they should go. Some are being overlaid on the actual baseball diamond, whereas others appear like electronic billboards on surfaces of the stadium. This new digital technology is just one example of new dynamic canvases to work with.

As new types of banner advertising appear on television programs, broadcasters are beginning to take advantage of the audience's ability to absorb simultaneous messages. Multiple promotions, brand identifications, and graphic overlays are now ubiquitous. With the government mandates for digital broadcasting, high-definition television will change what consumers see, and give creative work even more flexibility as it takes advantage of the new technology capabilities.

As the technology creates more possibilities for brand communications, we have to ask what is the most effective and efficient way to reach our target? Do you really want to see an advertisement for the CBS *Evening News with Dan Rather* printed on the back of a taxi receipt, as I recently did in San Francisco? Do ads for television programs work like stickers on bananas? Do we want to see advertising at gas stations? The variety of outlets is going to multiply like the number of infomercials promising you can lose weight without exercising. The brand message is going to be subject to a host of other issues, most of which will be beyond our control.

Even high-end cultural institutions have to deal with these issues. The familiar supertitles that appear in most opera houses (that instant-translation feature), was a point of turmoil at the Metropolitan Opera in New York, when it was thought inappropriate to subject the entire audience to supertitles. Why impose a change on your customers when many were paying for the experience precisely because there was no change? A solution was found in installing individual screens on the back of each seat, giving the audience the choice of individually watching or not watching the titles. How long will it be, though, before those small screens offer patrons information about upcoming events, or even special opportunities for them to buy more tickets? If, for example, each seat on an airline is being transformed into a personal digital world, with gambling, movies, and games, the messages that are created can't be dreamed up in a mass context. The creative expression of the brand communications is going to be both universal and personal.

With all these options available, brand builders face new challenges in their craft. That means the creative may have to be different for different audiences and different media, but they'll all have to have the same brand promise, the same brand message, and the same brand essence.

The new Rose Garden in Portland, Oregon, is already paving the way for the next-generation multimedia test lab. Home to the Portland Trailblazers basketball team, the arena is pushing ahead with individual digital monitors for spectators. The team's web site is already linked to player stats, schedules, fan e-mail subscriptions, as well as a connection to NBC, which broadcasts the games. You can even get ticket information through a link to Ticketmaster's web site. Of course, it helps that the team's owner is none other than Paul Allen, cofounder of Microsoft. It is, however, a telling report on the shift in how brand messages are going to be absorbed, when you realize the number of brand boundaries you are crossing when you check out a schedule, select seats, and pay for your tickets, all on-line. At the Rose Garden, the mass appeal of sports will be combined with individual options about team information, replays, and of course, ads. Those ads will all run at different times, and people will even have a choice of which ads to watch.

The Role of Agencies

With the megamergers in the 1980s, the ad agency world went through wrenching changes. Compensation was cut, client and agency churn increased, client relationships became less stable, our understanding of some great brands dissipated. The advertising community, client and agency alike, opted for transactions rather than relationships.

If agency people are going to have a better chance of predicting what will work with consumers, we're going to have to establish relationships that survive the failures of our creative work. Not all creative is going to be successful, but agency people have a better chance of understanding popular trends than marketing people laboring inside a corporate environment. We have to teach people to evaluate creative work not for how it moves on the screen, but how it moves the person who is going to buy. Breakthrough creative has to be so fresh, so relevant that it accomplishes its objective immediately. If not, it will have no impact—lost in the recycle bin or forgotten along with the other hundred or so messages consumers receive every day!

One of the biggest challenges in the creative process is suspending the desire for control. You can provide leadership around the brand and inspire great creative work that then inspires the consumer; however, you have to let go of the command-and-control concepts of managing the process. The biggest reason CEOs don't pay attention to branding isn't because they don't believe in the value of the brand; rather, it's because they can't control it. They want something rational and measurable. As a brand professional, you've got to have patience with them and build areas of trust so you can get to the point at which they say, "I don't understand, but I trust you." Talk about a breakthrough! If you are able to demonstrate that your goal is always to connect the brand to the ultimate consumer—you have a chance of making that breakthrough.

How can you get your organization to participate in great creative and successful brand building? You have to commit the entire organization. If brand strategy development is stuck in some powerless and invisible department of the company, it is not likely to have much impact. The essence of great brand strategy uncovers a real truth about the product or the service. Great brand strategies aren't about convincing people to buy one type of gasoline over another. They're about articulating fundamental relationships that touch us in ways that provide meaning and value to our lives. Great brands are about the total experience—everything you do as a company with your employees, your supplies, your channels, your partners, *and* your customers.

Our Shared Future

Everything I have discussed with you over the last ten chapters has been formed and informed by technology. Without technology, we would not have the pace of innovation we have today. Without that pace, we would not have the desire—no, the need—for faster time to market. Without information technology in particular, we would be unable to exchange important bits of information around the world in real time, the real enabler of warp-speed branding. Without the need for speed, we could merrily continue in our comfortable routines with our myths and mythologies, simply not accepting the fundamental ways in which our environments, our processes, and our consumers have changed.

My hope is that this book has helped you to reorganize and understand the many dynamics affecting your industry, and that with this heightened understanding, you will be better prepared to embrace your future with enthusiasm and much success.

Acknowledgments

Let me take this opportunity to thank, in a small way, the number of people who contributed to this book directly and indirectly.

I had been interested in taking the observations and experiences of the past decade and putting them to paper when Andrew Jaffe, the executive editor of *Adweek* magazine, heard me speak at an industry conference and suggested that I write for John Wiley & Sons. He introduced me to Senior Editor Ruth Mills, and the rest of the story lies in the pages before you. Many thanks to both Ruth and Andrew for their encouragement, support, and active feedback during the development of the book, making it stronger at every stage. A special thanks to Andrew Jaffe for his constructive inputs and the occasional kick in the pants to keep things moving.

A very special thanks goes to my colleague, Bill Green, without whom this book would have been very difficult to write. Bill has lived through many of the experiences that shaped my thinking, and he has participated in lively discussions over the years as our insights and observations about the changing world sharpened. We have had many heated debates over what was an anomaly and what was an emerging trend, and most important, what should we, as an advertising agency, do about it. When it came time to write these observations down, Bill became the institutional memory on which to draw for the best case histories, examples, and facts that proved the point. Bill, you have been a joy to work with over these past 10 years.

In addition to her regular responsibilities, Kimberly Edmondson, my executive assistant, took on the task of managing numerous revisions forwarded to her from ungodly places at strange hours of the day and night, collecting permissions to reproduce artwork (a full-time job in itself), and managing the flow of the book to meet all deadlines. Without her, we would be at least three drafts behind. Many thanks to Kimberly for her dedication and personal sense of pride in making this huge project come together.

Thank you to the staff of John Wiley & Sons, especially Kirsten Miller, editorial assistant, for the logistical support, to Brian Boucher for the cover design, and to Linda Witzling, associate managing editor. Many thanks also to Tom Laughman of North Market Street Graphics, my copy editor, for smoothing the rough edges.

Many colleagues and friends supplied facts and cases to make the points. Special thanks to John Elder of Goodby Silverstein and Partners, Cath Syme of Winkler Advertising, Jay Bain of Anderson Lembke, Renata Ritcheson of Dataquest, Michael Fineman of Fineman Associates Public Relations, Dana Sworakowski of Creative Cooking, Tom Carter and Mark Hyde of Lifeguard, Inc., Christina Avrett of TeamToolz and Pimm Fox. Their stories made the manuscript come alive.

Thanks to Frank Lewis and John Migliaccio (our creative directors) for their inputs on cover design and type treatment so that the book would be pleasant to read. Dave Bohn's illustrations made Chapter 3 come alive, as he does our presentations to clients. Thanks.

I would be remiss if I did not thank the early reviewers who read the first, very raw manuscript and gave me invaluable feedback and encouragement: Steve Weiss of Product Management Group, Jan Soderstrom of Visa International, Carol Lefcourt of the Lefcourt Group, Emil Regard of MySatellite, Steve Sarner of Travelscape, and Mike Kelly of Techtel. Finally, the last reviewers, who read the manuscript on short notice and prepared comments so that readers would have a better idea of what the book was about: Jan Soder-strom of Visa International, Paul Otellini of Intel Corp., Steve Weiss of the Product Management Group, Jim Kouzes of the Tom Peters Group/Learning Systems, and Carl Yankowski of Reebok International.

To complete the list, let me thank all the staff and clients of Winkler Advertising, without whose talents and creativity the observations in this book would not have been possible.

While I have this opportunity, I hope you will indulge me as I take a moment to acknowledge my parents, Wojciech and Halina Winkler. As underground freedom fighters against the Nazis during World War II, who had to escape from their native Poland to avoid persecution by the communists and make a new home in America, they taught me the meaning of character and courage. I would also like to acknowledge my husband, Art Lund, on whose love and support I depend every day. I'd like him to know—I'm back.

Credits

Volkswagen Think Small	With permission of Volkswagen of America.
Wendy's Where's the Beef?	With permission of Wendy's International.
American Express/ Hertz joint ad	With permission of American Express and Hertz.

Index

221

About the Author

Agnieszka Winkler is the founder and chief executive officer of Winkler Advertising, a leading San Francisco agency. Throughout her advertising career, Agnieszka has received many distinctions from both industry and civic organizations. Among them are Best Woman in Advertising, sponsored by *McCall's* magazine in conjunction with *Adweek* magazine; Ad Age's 100 Best and Brightest Women in Marketing and Advertising, Who's Who in Finance and Industry; Ad Age's 25 Women to Watch; the Who's Who of American Women, The International Directory of Distinguished Leadership; and many others. She received the Outstanding Alumni award from the Leavey School of Business at Santa Clara University in 1989, and she was the Santa Clara Graduate School of Business nominee for the Beta Gamma Sigma Medallion for Entrepreneurship.

Agnieszka's experience in advertising and branding has been sought after by companies on whose boards of directors she sits. Among them have been Lifeguard, Inc. (an HMO); RenoAir, until its purchase by American Airlines in late 1998, and Super-Cuts, until its purchase by Regis, Inc., both NASDAQ-listed companies; and the Board of Trustees of Santa Clara University.

She is a frequent speaker at industry meetings and business schools around the country on the subject of the impact of technology on marketing and advertising.

Most recently, Agnieszka founded TeamToolz, an Internet software company delivering products to recraft how marketing is done in the age of warp-speed branding.

Send me an e-mail:

E-mail: agnieszka@winklerad.com
Agnieszka Winkler
Winkler Advertising
301 Howard Street, 21st Floor
San Francisco, CA 94105

Dear Agnieszka:

Liked/didn't like the book overall

These ideas were especially helpful:

Have you considered:

Name:

Address:

Phone:

E-mail:

Other URLs to visit:

Winkler Advertising:	Winklerad.com
TeamToolz:	teamtoolz.com
Warp-speed branding:	warpspeedbranding.com